SpringerBriefs in Crimin

Policing

Series Editors

M.R. Haberfeld
City University of New York
John Jay College of Criminal Justice
New York, NY, USA

SpringerBriefs in Criminology present concise summaries of cutting edge research across the fields of Criminology and Criminal Justice. It publishes small but impactful volumes of between 50-125 pages, with a clearly defined focus. The series covers a broad range of Criminology research from experimental design and methods, to brief reports and regional studies, to policy-related applications.

The scope of the series spans the whole field of Criminology and Criminal Justice, with an aim to be on the leading edge and continue to advance research. The series will be international and cross-disciplinary, including a broad array of topics, including juvenile delinquency, policing, crime prevention, terrorism research, crime and place, quantitative methods, experimental research in criminology, research design and analysis, forensic science, crime prevention, victimology, criminal justice systems, psychology of law, and explanations for criminal behavior.

SpringerBriefs in Criminology will be of interest to a broad range of researchers and practitioners working in Criminology and Criminal Justice Research and in related academic fields such as Sociology, Psychology, Public Health, Economics and Political Science.

More information about this series at http://www.springer.com/series/11179

Georgios Leventakis • M. R. Haberfeld
Editors

Societal Implications of Community-Oriented Policing and Technology

 Springer Open

Editors
Georgios Leventakis
Senior Advisor - European Projects
Center for Security Studies - KEMEA
Hellenic Ministry of Interior - Public
Order Sector
Athens, Greece

M. R. Haberfeld
City University of New York
John Jay College of Criminal Justice
New York, NY, USA

ISSN 2192-8533   ISSN 2192-8541   (electronic)
SpringerBriefs in Criminology
ISSN 2194-6213   ISSN 2194-6221   (electronic)
SpringerBriefs in Policing
ISBN 978-3-319-89296-2   ISBN 978-3-319-89297-9   (eBook)
https://doi.org/10.1007/978-3-319-89297-9

Library of Congress Control Number: 2018940540

© The Editor(s) (if applicable) and The Author(s) 2018. This book is an open access publication.
Open Access This book is licensed under the terms of the Creative Commons Attribution 4.0
International License (http://creativecommons.org/licenses/by/4.0/), which permits use, sharing,
adaptation, distribution and reproduction in any medium or format, as long as you give appropriate credit
to the original author(s) and the source, provide a link to the Creative Commons license and indicate if
changes were made.
The images or other third party material in this book are included in the book's Creative Commons
license, unless indicated otherwise in a credit line to the material. If material is not included in the book's
Creative Commons license and your intended use is not permitted by statutory regulation or exceeds the
permitted use, you will need to obtain permission directly from the copyright holder.
The use of general descriptive names, registered names, trademarks, service marks, etc. in this publication
does not imply, even in the absence of a specific statement, that such names are exempt from the relevant
protective laws and regulations and therefore free for general use.
The publisher, the authors and the editors are safe to assume that the advice and information in this book
are believed to be true and accurate at the date of publication. Neither the publisher nor the authors or the
editors give a warranty, express or implied, with respect to the material contained herein or for any errors
or omissions that may have been made. The publisher remains neutral with regard to jurisdictional claims
in published maps and institutional affiliations.

Printed on acid-free paper

This Springer imprint is published by the registered company Springer International Publishing AG
part of Springer Nature.
The registered company address is: Gewerbestrasse 11, 6330 Cham, Switzerland

Acknowlegment

The work presented in this Brief received funding from the European Commission, under the:

- FP7-Security Topic SEC-2013-1.6-4 – Information Exploitation/Integration Project entitled **VALCRI** (Visual Analytics for Sense-Making in Criminal Intelligence Analysis) under grant agreement number FP7-IP-608142.
- "Ethical/Societal Dimension Topic H2020-fct-14-2014: TOPIC Enhancing cooperation between law enforcement agencies and citizens – Community policing" entitled **TRILLION** (Trusted, Citizen – LEA collaboration over sOcial Networks) under grant agreement number 653256.
- "H2020-FCT-2014 Ethical/Societal Dimension Topic 2: Enhancing cooperation between law enforcement agencies and citizens – Community policing" call entitled **INSPEC²T** (Inspiring CitizeNS Participation for Enhanced Community PoliCing AcTions) under grant agreement number 653749.
- "Societal Challenge: Safeguarding Secure Societies" Topic H2020-FCT-2014-2015/ H2020-FCT-2014: TOPIC "Ethical/Societal Dimension Topic 2: Enhancing cooperation between law enforcement agencies and citizens – Community policing" entitled **CITYCOP** (Citizen Interaction Technologies yield community policing) under grant agreement number 653811.
- "Societal Challenge: Safeguarding Secure Societies" Topic H2020-FCT-2014-2015/H2020-FCT-2014: TOPIC "Ethical/Societal Dimension Topic 2: Enhancing cooperation between law enforcement agencies and citizens – Community policing" entitled **UNITY** under grant agreement number 653729.

We also thank the following people for their great contributions to the success of this publication starting with the KEMEA member, Mr. Panayiotis Papanikolaou, whose technological and organization skills have no match; Katherine Chabalko from Springer whose vision for progressive information sharing has no bounds; and last but not least, Mr. Joseph Quatela, our production manager, whose dedication and assistance are unparalleled.

Georgios Leventakis and M. R. Haberfeld

Contents

About the Editors

Georgios Leventakis is a qualified Security Expert. He holds a PhD in the area of risk assessment modeling in critical infrastructure (CI) protection, an MBA, and an MSc in risk management. He has 22 years of professional experience in the public sector, of which 16 years are in security management. He has participated in several national, European, and international projects and initiatives regarding physical security of critical infrastructures, border management (land and sea border surveillance), and civil protection/homeland security technology and operations. He has also participated in tender procedures for complex security systems, including command and control and decision support systems.

His research interests include social media platforms in community policing, risk assessment modeling in CI protection, smart borders applications and tools, and integrated border management solutions. Since 2006, he was the scientific coordinator of the Center for Security Studies – the Scientific, Advisory and Research Center of the Hellenic Ministry of Interior (KEMEA) – and participated in various European programs funded by the European Commission. He has participated as senior researcher in more than 45 EU research projects, has authored several academic papers published in relevant journals, and has presented them at academic conferences.

Dr. Leventakis has worked and collaborated with many public safety and security agencies in Greece and abroad: from the planning phase of the Security Program for the ATHENS 2004 Olympic Games till more recently on the design and development of National Table Top and Operational Readiness Exercises. He has been involved in the development of **threat assessment and vulnerability assessment studies, operational security plans and emergency response plans, and procedures for the protection of vital infrastructures and governmental buildings in Greece and EU.** He has clearance to handle classified documents up to "Top Secret" level.

M. R. Haberfeld is Professor of Police Science in the Department of Law, Police Science and Criminal Justice Administration at John Jay College of Criminal Justice in New York City. She holds a PhD in Criminal Justice from City University of New York (CUNY), two Master degrees (one from CUNY and one from the Hebrew University), and two Bachelor of Arts degrees from the Hebrew University in Jerusalem. She was born in Poland and immigrated to Israel as a teenager. She served in the Israeli Defense Forces in a counterterrorist unit and left the army at the rank of a sergeant. Prior to coming to United States, she served in the Israel National Police and left the force at the rank of lieutenant. She also worked as a special consultant for the US Drug Enforcement Administration in the New York Field Office.

She has conducted research in the areas of public and private law enforcement, police integrity, counterterrorism, and white-collar crime in the United States, Eastern and Western Europe, and Israel. In addition to her research, she has also provided leadership and counterterrorist training to a number of police agencies and military units across the United States and a number of countries around the world. Since 2001 she has been involved in developing, coordinating, and teaching in a special educational program at John Jay College designed, exclusively, for the sworn members of the New York City Police Department. She has recently developed an online Certificate for Law Enforcement Leadership offered by the John Jay College.

Her publications include numerous authored, coauthored, and coedited books, chapters, and briefs, among them three books are on terrorism-related issues: *A New Understanding of Terrorism* (coeditor, 2010), *Modern Piracy and Maritime Terrorism* (coeditor, 2012), and *Terrorism Within Comparative International Context* (coauthor, 2009); *Russian Organized Corruption Networks and Their International Trajectories* (coauthored, 2011), *Critical Issues in Police Training* (2013; 2018), *Police Organization and Training: Innovations in Research and Practice* (coedited, 2011), *Police Leadership: Organizational and Managerial Decision Making Process* (2012), *Policing Muslim Communities* (coauthored, 2012), *Match-Fixing in International Sports* (coedited, 2013), *Introduction to Policing: The Pillar of Democracy* (coauthored, 2014, 2017), and *Measuring Police Integrity Across the World* (coedited, 2015). She is also an editor of SpringerBriefs in Policing.

Contributors

Ben Brewster CENTRIC – Centre of Excellence in Terrorism, Resilience, Intelligence and Organised Crime Research, Sheffield Hallam University, Sheffield, UK

Christina Charitou University of West Attica, Electronics Engineering Department, Egaleo, Greece

Ioana Cristina Cotoi Engineering Ingegneria, Informatica, SPA, Lecce, Italy

Janina Czapska Department of Sociology of Law, Faculty of Law, Jagiellonian University, Kraków, Poland

P. Duquenoy Middlesex University, London, UK

G. Galdon Clavell Eticas Research & Consulting, Barcelona, Spain

Helen Gibson CENTRIC – Centre of Excellence in Terrorism, Resilience, Intelligence and Organised Crime Research, Sheffield Hallam University, Sheffield, UK

D. Gotterbarn Software Engineering Ethics Research Institute, Department of Computing, East Tennessee State University, Johnson City, Tennessee, USA

Mike Gunning CENTRIC – Centre of Excellence in Terrorism, Resilience, Intelligence and Organised Crime Research, Sheffield Hallam University, Sheffield, UK

M. R. Haberfeld City University of New York, John Jay College of Criminal Justice, New York, NY, USA

Jarmo Houtsonen Police University College, Tampere, Finland

Vesa Huotari Police University College, Tampere, Finland

Pirjo Jukarainen Police University College, Tampere, Finland

K. K. Kimppa University of Turku, Turku, Finland

Neesha Kodagoda Middlesex University, London, UK

Dimitrios G. Kogias University of West Attica, Electronics Engineering Department, Egaleo, Greece

Olavi Kujanpää Police University College, Tampere, Finland

John L. M. McDaniel School of Social, Historical and Political Studies, Mary Seacole Building, University of Wolverhampton, Wolverhampton, UK

Julia Muraszkiewicz Trilateral Research Ltd, London, UK

Johannes Pieter Oosthuizen University of Winchester, Winchester, UK

N. Patrignani Universita Cattolicà del Sacro Cuore, Milan, Italy

Charalampos Z. Patrikakis University of West Attica, Electronics Engineering Department, Egaleo, Greece

Nickolaos Petropoulos City University of New York, John Jay College of Criminal Justice, New York, NY, USA

Spyros E. Polykalas TEI of Ionian Islands, Digital Media and Communication Department, Kefallonia, Greece

Chris Rooney Middlesex University, London, UK

Patrick Seidler Middlesex University, London, UK

Katarzyna Struzińska Department of Sociology of Law, Faculty of Law, Jagiellonian University, Kraków, Poland

Jari Taponen Police University College, Tampere, Finland

Alison Wakefield University of Portsmouth, Portsmouth, UK

B. L. William Wong Middlesex University, London, UK

M. M. Zamorano Eticas Research & Consulting, Barcelona, Spain

J. M. Zavala Pérez Eticas Research & Consulting, Barcelona, Spain

Chapter 1
Supporting Variability in Criminal Intelligence Analysis: From Expert Intuition to Critical and Rigorous Analysis

B. L. William Wong, Patrick Seidler, Neesha Kodagoda, and Chris Rooney

Introduction

Analysts in criminal intelligence analysis regularly face data from multiple sources that are often incomplete, possibly deceptive, un-reliable and messy. This creates situations with high uncertainty and ambiguity, which makes the generation of plausible, reliable arguments difficult or impossible. However, many visual analytics and machine learning systems require that data for analysis be available, with the system substituting, for example, system averages for missing data. This makes it difficult for analysts to deal with the reality of facing deceptive and missing data. Failures in the assessment of criminal situations or the inability to come to a conclusion as the result of an analytical process can lead to severe consequences. A lack of awareness, overlooking or not realising the need to locate a key piece of information because one does not know the data exist can also lead to human errors. One solution to this problem is the facilitation of storytelling. Storytelling requires data to be assembled and organised to tell a story that explains a situation or phenomenon. By externalising and making the storytelling process visible and tangible to the analyst via a computer display, it becomes possible for the analyst to inspect his or her own reasoning processes. This creates the possibility to check one's analyses and assumptions for omissions and contradictions. Analysts need a kind of user interface that allows them to easily explore different ways to organise and sequence existing data into plausible stories or explanations that can eventually evolve into narratives that bind the data together into a formal explanation. If an analyst is presented with limited data or even no data, then such a tool must allow the analyst to easily make assumptions and suppositions that could be used to initiate a line of inquiry or connect separate pieces of data to concoct a plausible explanation.

B. L. William Wong (✉) · P. Seidler · N. Kodagoda · C. Rooney
Middlesex University, London, UK
e-mail: w.wong@mdx.ac.uk

© The Author(s) 2018
G. Leventakis, M. R. Haberfeld (eds.), *Societal Implications of Community-Oriented Policing and Technology*, SpringerBriefs in Criminology,
https://doi.org/10.1007/978-3-319-89297-9_1

In this paper we describe the user interface for storytelling in a new criminal intelligence analysis system prototype and the principled basis for its design. In this interface, information (e.g. a report, snippets of the report, statistical analyses) are represented in tile-like interface objects that can be freely moved around like playing cards on a table top. Interacting through a multi-touch display, analysts can manipulate and freely arrange the information cards into meaningful sequences to create explanations. We also discuss the variety of thinking strategies in the storytelling and analytic reasoning process, and how it may be supported through the application of the Fluidity and Rigour Model.

Fluidity and Rigour

The Fluidity and Rigour Model, see Fig. 1.1, or FRM Wong (2016), is a model intended for interaction designers. It highlights the variability of analytic reasoning strategies employed by analysts during criminal intelligence and investigative analysis, and describes the range of visualisation and interaction methods needed for criminal intelligence analysis systems.

The reasoning strategies invoked by analysts range from making guesses and suppositions that enable storytelling when very little is known, to reasoning strategies that lead to rigorous and systematic evaluation of explanations that have been created through the analytic process. In the FRM, we define fluidity as the ease by which a system can be used to support the variability of thinking strategies expressed

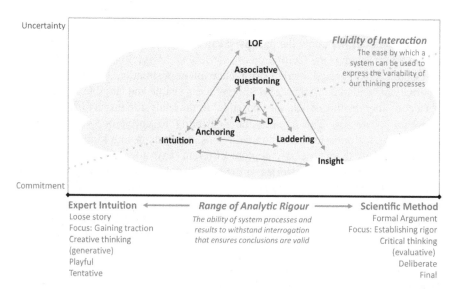

Fig. 1.1 Fluidity and rigour model. Legend: inference making: induction (I), deduction (D) and abduction (A); user strategies: anchoring, laddering, associative question; cognitive acts: intuition, LOF (Leap of Faith), and insight

in the analytic reasoning process; and by rigour we mean the extent to which analytic methods and processes produce results and conclusions that are valid and can stand up to interrogation.

Sources of Variability in Analytic Reasoning

The Law of Requisite Variety, states that "... *R's capacity as a regulator cannot exceed its capacity as a channel for variety*" (Ashby 1958). Re-stated, "... the variety of variability of a process to be controlled must be matched or exceeded by the variety of variability of the controlling entity...". This refers to the variety of situations a system designed to control or support a process must be capable of controlling or supporting. The lack of compatibility between the variety of situations a process can produce, and the ability of a controlling system to support or accommodate that variety will invariably lead to system failures or sub-optimal performance. Systems designed to support intelligence analysis need to support not only the observable tasks of information search and retrieval and data analysis, but also the much less observable but crucial thinking and reasoning processes. These are the cognitive processes that determine the logic and how sensible are the narratives created to explain the clues that present themselves in an investigation.

Analysts make use of various inference making strategies – induction, deduction and abduction – depending upon what data they have, the rules for interpreting the data they are starting with, and the conclusions they would make or would like to make (Wong and Kodagoda 2016). The early stages of an investigation are often characterised by a lack of information and the need to imaginatively create plausible stories or explanations, such as abductive inferences to initiate possible lines of inquiry. Analysts also practise a mix of critical thinking and storytelling. In this process they elaborate, question, and often reframe and discard explanations (Klein et al. 2007), with some evolving into stronger, well-justified explanations that are robust enough to withstand interrogation (Rooney et al. 2014). Wong and Kodagoda (2016) present other aspects of the analytical reasoning process: anchoring, laddering, and posing associative questions. Analysts engage in a process of anchoring to gain traction and initiate inquiry. They then engage in a laddering process where they develop explanations to extend or elaborate their ideas into new understanding. They complement the anchoring and laddering activities by associative questioning to discover what else might exists. Police analysts are taught, for example, the 5WH model – who, what, where, when, why and how – to activate divergent thinking pathways that may lead to un-expected associations; which through intuition, could spur the recognition of un-anticipated patterns (Gerber et al. 2016) across different data sets. Often the problem is not 'joining the dots' – but to imagine more informative ways to connect them to create better insights under information-sparse, uncertain, and ambiguous conditions. This requires some degree of creativity when trying to imagine plausible explanations, and for getting the cognitive traction required for gaining further insight.

We use the x-axis of Fig. 1.1 to illustrate the range of analytic rigour that may be applied to the analytic reasoning process. At the start of an inquiry there is usually very little known about a case. It is therefore of little use to treat information and inferences rigorously as the analyst is still trying to understand what the data means and whether it is sensible to create an argument. The type of thinking and reasoning employed by the analyst at this stage may be characterised as being creative, having to deal with high uncertainty as there are many unknowns and missing data. The need at this stage is to gain traction and to get the investigation started. Analysts engage in the tentative and playful generation of plausible stories and hypotheses that may account for their observations. They tend not to commit to a single explanation and are likely to explore alternatives.

At the high rigour end of the spectrum, the type of thinking and reasoning required may be characterised as 'critical thinking', evaluative, deliberate, and final. As an investigation approaches the closing stages, most of the data required will be known. It is then possible to rigorously structure, organise, or analyse the data, and to make sure that every conceivable logical discussion can be evaluated. By this stage, analysts would have employed a variety of structured analytic techniques (see for example, Heuer and Pherson 2014) to establish strong and rigorous arguments. Then usually having done all the analyses and checks – would be committed to an explanation.

Fluidity to Interact with the Variety of Analytic Tools

Fluidity is the ease by which a system can be used to support the variability of thinking strategies demonstrated by analysts in the analytic reasoning process (Wong 2016). To achieve this, the interaction and visualisation methods need to enable the analyst to seamlessly transition within and between the tools needed by the different analytical reasoning strategies. Elmqvist et al. (2011) has explained that the basic requirement for fluidity is for users to feel that they are directly participating in the interface, where users feel that are able "… to directly 'touch' and manipulate the visualization instead of indirectly conversing with a user interface". Fluidity in a user interface therefore "… involves achieving a sense of immersion, a first-personness and direct engagement with the objects and the visualizations" creating an embodiment with the user interface to create a sense of 'being in the flow', directly benefiting analytic performance (Bederson 2004). Pike et al. (2009) advocates that visual displays must be "embedded in an interactive framework that scaffolds the human knowledge construction process with the right tools and methods to support the accumulation of evidence and observations into theories and beliefs". To achieve this level of interactivity, we also ensure that real-time responses are close to the 100 ms recommendation (Kalawsky 2009). The aim is to create a tight loop between query and analysis to support Neisser's (1976) perception-action cycle to achieve a level of engagement that may be interpreted as a real-time dialogue between the user and the machine. Impediments in the interaction would obstruct the analytic discourse (Dykes 2005), making the interface frustrating to use, leading to higher cognitive loads, activation of cognitive biases (Munzner 2014), and poorer situation awareness.

Requirements for Fluidity and Rigor

In what ways might technology assist in supporting the variability of the analytic reasoning process? Based on a number of studies we conducted: e.g. focus group studies with 20 intelligence analysts (Wong and Varga 2012); think-aloud studies with analysts and librarians performing simulated intelligence tasks (Rooney et al. 2014; Kodagoda et al. 2013); and cognitive task analyses with analysts from three major police forces in Europe (e.g. Wong and Kodagoda 2016; Gerber et al. 2016), we summarise below the key design requirements for fluidity in analytical reasoning.

The tools at the 'loose story' end of the rigour spectrum should be different from the tools supporting more rigorous approaches on the other end of the spectrum. At the 'loose story' end, the tools should enable the analyst to express the *creative, generative, chaotic and tentative* nature of reasoning by enabling *playful experimentation* that is needed for one to *gain cognitive traction* with which to start an idea to pursue a line of investigation. It should facilitate *associative and divergent* thinking by anticipating and presenting information that might be needed next. We next focus on how analysts can transition fluidly between critical thinking methods, and methods for creative exploration, hypotheses formulation, and storytelling. The tools should enable the analysts to *transition seamlessly* from early analyses that led to tentative possibilities, to *assemble* data and *ground* the explanations so that *narratives* could be developed into strong arguments. Analysts should also be able to transition fluidly between different forms and assemblies of explanations, outcomes, assessments, and analyses, to uncover other possibilities that may lie with in the data.

Operationalising Fluidity and Rigour

The design requirements summarised above have been implemented in the VALCRI prototype – Visual Analytics for Sense-making in Criminal Intelligence Analysis. The aim of the VALCRI project is to create an integrated visual analytics-based sense-making capability for criminal intelligence analysis that facilitates human reasoning and analytic discourse by being tightly coupled with semi-automated machine learning knowledge extraction technologies. This tight coupling enables VALCRI to respond to analysts in both a proactive and reactive manner. The design of VALCRI is based on the idea of a Joint Cognitive System. Rather than humans just working and interfacing better with technology, the intention is to create a system of human-machine co-agency where the human-machine team "can modify its behaviour on the basis of experience so as to achieve specific anti-entropic ends" (Hollnagel and Woods 2005) (p. 22). Johansson (2014) explains that to achieve such anti-entropic ends requires that systems abide by the Law of Requisite Variety, i.e. the system need to have the repertoire of methods for dealing with the variety of behaviours that the environment is likely to produce. To implement fluidity the interactions and visualisations enable the analyst to fluidly make transitions within and between the variety of analytic reasoning tasks. Visualisations that enable fluidity are those that, for example, morph from one representation format suitable for one task, and with minimal or no effort nor interruptions, into another. Interactions that enable fluidity enable effortless transitions between different states or representational formats of the data. In VALCRI this occurs when a user clicks or drags a specific dot in a scatter plot diagram and it immediately retrieves and presents the full crime report it represents. We next outline how these requirements have informed VALCRI designs.

Visual Persistence

Persistence occurs when data and the state of one's analysis and reasoning are made visible and remains in view. It enables the analyst to off-load memory challenging activities such as recalling facts to the interface. The VALCRI user interface design is based on the concept of the Thinking Landscape that comprises a flexible set of structured spaces. Analysts can externalise their thinking and leverage human spatial memory. Analysts can maintain the visibility of the storytelling process while concurrently working on different explanatory assemblies in the user interface. As in a landscape, nearby spaces enable one to see detail, while farther away spaces provide a sense of context. We introduce three main areas of work for the analyst: Places nearby to 'Assemble and Construct'; places to 'Park and Mull' are slightly further away, with information reduced or summarized so that incomplete ideas or partial explanations can be 'parked' temporarily where the analyst is still able to quickly continue to pursue them; and a Place for Context where situational and contextual information are located.

Tactile Reasoning for Tentative and Playful Interactions

We define tactile reasoning as an interaction technique that supports analytical reasoning by the direct manipulation of information objects in the graphical user interface (Takken and Wong 2015). Just as the alphabet tiles used in the game of 'Scrabble', VALCRI uses tiles to represent pieces of information such as crime reports, and stop and search reports. These tiles can be directly and freely manipulated, moved and arranged. Explained as epistemic actions (Kirsh 1995; Kirsh and

Maglio 1994), these actions assist the analysts to modify their work environment to support the externalisation of their thinking and reasoning processes. This externalisation makes the complex mental tasks during investigative decision making tractable. The design of the interaction methods and how the information and tiles are visualised and laid out have been based on a variety of human factors principles (e.g. Emergent Features, Gestalt, Proximity-Compatibility). By coupling tactile reasoning with underlying machine learning functions, we enable reactive and proactive actions, e.g. to search for crime reports with similar characteristics in response to a direct request, or a search in advance of a request as the analyst works through an analysis. This enables the kind of analytic discourse that can potentially assist analysts discover new relationships.

Tactile reasoning supports the process of playful storytelling. It allows the analyst to create tentative sequences of data from which narratives might emerge. The information tiles and tile containing results from data analysis in the storytelling workspace can be freely re-organised to communicate different explanations. Intelligence analysts face many tedious and repetitive tasks, such as the reading and selection of crime reports to systematically extract common concepts to create a summary table to perform a Comparative Crime Analysis (National Policing Improvement Agency 2008). In VALCRI, the analyst can fluidly make the transition from playful storytelling to rigorous analysis with one click, eliminating many of the repetitive intermediate cut and paste steps.

Creative and Generative

The usual starting point for investigations in VALCRI is a search. The design enables multiple searches to be initialised on a single canvas. Results may be analysed in the 'Assemble and Construct' place, or parked in the 'Park and Mull' places. This enables the analyst to conduct multiple independent searches, giving the analyst freedom to creatively pursue alternative pathways, while organising the search space to cater for one's thinking and reasoning approach. The VALCRI user interface is customisable and based on the principle of dynamic visual querying (Shneiderman 1994), enabling the analyst to gain an "overview first, zoom and filter, then details-on-demand" (Shneiderman 1996). Filtering in VALCRI has been implemented via direct interaction of data in multiple coordinated views. For example, crime reports may be presented within the boundaries of a zoomed-in map. By changing one view, e.g. the boundaries of the map view, the system will present a revised set of crime reports on the map, a revised timeline view comprising the corresponding data, or a revised summary table of the crime reports. This provides the analysts with easy access to alternative perspectives that may be playfully and tentatively investigated without having to redefine their search from scratch each time.

Because of uncertainty and ambiguity in intelligence analysis, analysts often need to playfully experiment with data to generate hypotheses and explanations based on little or no information. One approach to gain traction is to create anchors that enable new ideas about the kinds of actions that one can take (Klein 2014, p. 148). In addition, VALCRI design encourages the use of imagination to generate new possibilities, ideas or concepts beyond what is presented. Kodagoda et al. (2013) discovered that during the early stages of analysis, once the participants discovered patterns or semantically meaningful connections in the data set, they were able to identify anchors from which to spawn new searches.

Associative and Divergent

Insight pathways can also be activated through divergent thinking. This involves retrieving data that could be associated in some way and then by presenting such data together in the same visual space, analyst may activate unanticipated associations. For example, by presenting information about solved and unsolved crimes in a given district in the same visual space, we create opportunities for analysts to ask questions about similar crimes, or whether the offenders and their known co-offenders could have committed some of crimes that are currently unsolved? In this way, we create opportunities for the human to make plausible links – associations – that may not be possible or feasible for the computer to predict.

Gaining Traction During Uncertainty

Uncertainty in the analytical process poses a major risk for the analyst to miss information and can quickly lead to errors. In VALCRI, we have taken the approach of turning uncertainty into opportunities for the analyst to ask questions. For example, due to the way information is recorded in police systems, the same person can be registered under different reference numbers, and different spellings of names (e.g. Smith vs. Smythe). Most analysts address this problem with prior knowledge or experience. For such problems, VALCRI can provide sets of certain and uncertain matches for the analysts to compare and to assess for themselves the correctness and relevance of the data. This way, we make the analyst aware of information that can immediately confirm or explain ambiguities. Another type of uncertainty stems from the un-awareness that there are missing data. One method to address the missing data problem was proposed in Wong and Varga (2012), called 'black holes', or gaps in a sequence of data. These gaps or black holes create opportunities for the analyst to ask "why?"; why was there a gap in activities between this time to that time? Did our sensors fail to pick up the events? Did the criminals go into hiding and initiated a 'radio silence' procedure? In VALCRI, analysts can choose to show or not show the black holes in data represented in timeline sequences or story sequences based on laws of argumentation.

Conclusion

Intelligence analysts frequently find themselves in situations of high uncertainty and ambiguity. The characteristics of these situations force the analyst to rely on creative generation of plausible explanations – 'storytelling'. We suggested that current interaction design approaches obstruct the storytelling process and impede analysts in performing well in their analytical reasoning process.

In this paper, we presented and discussed the Fluidity and Rigour Model (Wong 2016) as an approach for combining storytelling with the interaction methods that are needed to support the variety of reasoning and thinking strategies involved in the investigative and analytic process. We commonly regard analytic reasoning – the thinking, cognitive acts and inferential strategies we use in the tradecraft of intelligence analysis – as mainly requiring structured, critical and rigorous analysis methods (Heuer and Pherson 2014). While absolutely essential, we have neglected the fact that investigators and analysts also engage in a considerable level of abductive inferential reasoning (Josephson and Tanner 1996; Walton 2005) that is speculative and tentative, to generate plausible explanations that provide a basis for formulating an initial hypothesis that can be subsequently tested. This process draws very much on the analysts' expert intuition to make leaps of faith that may lead to moments of insights that enable the making of suppositions. In this paper we do not advocate systems design that support either one extreme or the other. Instead, we propose that it is important to support both extremes of analytic reasoning. It is vitally important that we make it possible for the analysts to employ their expert intuition while recognising the limits of it; and to make it possible for them to fluidly transition to scientific methods, with an emphasis on empirical testing and peer review. We believe the Fluidity and Rigour Model of interaction design, provides one approach that can guide the design of systems capable of supporting such variability.

We also discussed the Law of Requisite Variety. Failing to achieve such a level of compatiblity between the variability in the processes we wish to suuport and the systems we design to support them, especially in the context of intelligence analysis, the systems we produce will continue to be inadequate for supporting the variability of thinking and reasoning strategies invoked by investigators and intelligence analysts.

Acknowledgements The research leading to the results reported in this paper received funding from the European Union 7th Framework Programme through Project VALCRI under the EC Grant Agreement N° FP7-SEC-IP-608142 awarded to B.L. William Wong, Middlesex University London, and partners.

References

Ashby, W. R. (1958). Requisite variety and its implications for the control of complex systems. *Cybernetica, 1*(2), 83–99.
Bederson, B. B. (2004). Interfaces for staying in the flow. *Ubiquity, 2004*(September), 1–8.

Dykes, J. (2005). Facilitating interaction for geo-visualisation. In J. Dykes, A. M. MacEachren, & M.-J. Kraak (Eds.), *Exploring geovisualization* (pp. 265–292). Amsterdam: Elsevier.

Elmqvist, N., Moere, A. V., Jetter, H.-C., Cernea, D., Reiterer, H., & Jankun-Kelly, T. (2011). Fluid interaction for information visualization. *Information Visualization, 10*(4), 327–340.

Gerber, M., Wong, B. L. W., & Kodagoda, N. (2016). How analysts think: Intuition, leap of faith and insight. In *In proceedings of the human factors and ergonomics society 60th annual meeting* (Vol. 60, p. 173). Washington, DC: SAGE Publications.

Heuer, R. J. J., & Pherson, R. H. (2014). *Structured analytic techniques for intelligence analysis* (2nd ed.). Los Angeles, CA: SAGE CQ Press.

Hollnagel, E., & Woods, D. D. (2005). *Joint cognitive systems: Foundations of cognitive systems engineering*. Boca Raton, FL: CRC Press, Taylor and Francis Group, LLC.

Johansson, B. J. E. (2014). Agility in Command and Control - Functional Models of Cognition. In E. Svensson, S. Nählinder, & P. Berggren (Eds.), *Assessing Command and Control Effectiveness: Dealing with a Changing World* (pp. 177–192). Farnham, England: Ashgate Publishing, Ltd.

Josephson, J. R., & Tanner, M. C. (1996). Conceptual analysis of abduction. In J. R. Josephson & S. G. Josephson (Eds.), *Abductive inference: Computation, philosophy, technology*. Cambridge: Cambridge University Press.

Kalawsky, R. S. (2009). Gaining greater insight through interactive visualization: A human factors perspective. In R. Liere, T. Adriaansen, & E. Zudilova-Seinstra (Eds.), *Trends in interactive visualization* (pp. 119–154). London: Springer.

Kirsh, D. (1995). Complementary strategies: Why we use our hands when we think. Paper presented at the seventeenth annual conference of the cognitive science society, July 22-25, 1995, University of Pittsburgh.

Kirsh, D., & Maglio, P. (1994). On distinguishing epistemic from pragmatic action. *Cognitive Science, 18*(4), 513–549.

Klein, G. (2014). *Seeing what others don't: The remarkable ways we gain insights. London, England: Nicholas Brealey Publishing.Nicholas Brealey Publishing* 2014. London: England.

Klein, G., Philips, J. K., Rall, E. L., & Peluso, D. A. (2007). A data-frame theory of sense-making. In R. R. Hoffman (Ed.), *Expertise Out of Context: Proceedings of the Sixth International Conference on Naturalistic Decision Making* (pp. 113–155). New York: Lawrence Erlbaum Associates.

Kodagoda, N., Attfield, S., Wong, B. L. W., Rooney, C., & Choudhury, T. (2013). Using Interactive Visual Reasoning to Support Sense-making: Implications for Design. *IEEE Transactions on Visualization and Computer Graphics, 19*(12), 2217–2226.

Munzner, T. (2014). *Visualization analysis and design*. Boca Raton: A K Peters/CRC Press.

National Policing Improvement Agency. (2008). *Practice Advice on Analysis*. Specialist Operations Centre, Wyboston Lakes, Bedfordshire, UK: Association of Chief Police Officers.

Neisser, U. (1976). *Cognition and reality*. New York, NY: W.H. Freeman and Company.

Pike, W. A., Stasko, J., Chang, R., & O'Connell, T. A. (2009). The science of interaction. *Information Visualization, 8*(4), 263–274.

Rooney, C., Attfield, S., Wong, B. L. W., & Choudhury, S. (2014). INVISQUE as a tool for intelligence analysis: The construction of explanatory narratives. *International Journal of Human–Computer Interaction, 30*(9), 703–717.

Shneiderman, B. (1994). Dynamic queries for visual information seeking. *IEEE Software, 11*(6), 70–77.

Shneiderman, B. (1996). The eyes have it: A task by data type taxonomy for information visualizations. In *Proceedings 1996 IEEE Symposium on Visual Languages* (pp. 336–343).

Takken, S., & Wong, B. L. W. (2015). Tactile reasoning: Hands-on vs. Hands-off – What's the difference? *Cognition, Technology & Work, 17*(3), 381–390. https://doi.org/10.1007/s10111-015-0331-5.

Walton, D. N. (2005). *Abductive reasoning*. Tuscaloosa, Alabama: The University of Alambam Press.

Wong, B. L. W. (2016). Fluidity and rigour: Addressing the design considerations for OSINT tools and processes. In B. Akhgar, P. S. Bayerl, & F. Sampson (Eds.), *Open source intelligence investigation: From strategy to implementation* (pp. 167–189). Cham, Switzeland: Springer International Publishing AG.

Wong, B. L. W., & Kodagoda, N. (2016). How analysts think: Anchoring, laddering and associations. *Proceedings of the Human Factors and Ergonomics Society Annual Meeting, 60*(1), 178–182.

Wong, B. L. W., & Varga, M. (2012). Black holes, keyholes and Brown worms: Challenges in sense making. *Proceedings of the Human Factors and Ergonomics Society Annual Meeting, 56*(1), 287–291.

Open Access This chapter is licensed under the terms of the Creative Commons Attribution 4.0 International License (http://creativecommons.org/licenses/by/4.0/), which permits use, sharing, adaptation, distribution and reproduction in any medium or format, as long as you give appropriate credit to the original author(s) and the source, provide a link to the Creative Commons license and indicate if changes were made.

The images or other third party material in this chapter are included in the chapter's Creative Commons license, unless indicated otherwise in a credit line to the material. If material is not included in the chapter's Creative Commons license and your intended use is not permitted by statutory regulation or exceeds the permitted use, you will need to obtain permission directly from the copyright holder.

Chapter 2
Strategic Analysis and Service Design for Community Policing

Olavi Kujanpää, Pirjo Jukarainen, Jari Taponen, Jarmo Houtsonen, and Vesa Huotari

Introduction

Police services around the world have been in turmoil at the twenty-first century. Structures have been reorganized, budgets cut and reservations expressed about the traditional approaches to policing (e.g. Fyfe et al. 2013). At the same time evidence-based, intelligence-led and increasingly professional approaches have captivated reformers everywhere (e.g. Den Boer 2014). Furthermore, a security architecture, in which the police have played the leading role, seems to be gradually supplemented by a mosaic of security and safety service providers, collaborative arrangements, networks and partnerships (e.g. Hoogenboom 2010). New forms of networks, nodal governance and pluralistic systems (Frevel and Rogers 2016; Shearing and Johnston 2010; White 2011) are viewed as more agile, less costly and more responsive in resolving security problems than the old bureaucratic and centralized forms of governance.

Although the debates about the optimal arrangements for organizing policing are far from conclusive, there is an emerging agreement that policing should become more learning- and problem-oriented and community- and collaboration-based. However, there is uncertainty what these mean in terms of police strategy and daily practice. The purpose of this paper is to highlight what problem-oriented and collaboration-based approach demand from a Community Policing (CP) strategy. To begin with, we introduce different facets of the strategy and discuss how strategic

O. Kujanpää · P. Jukarainen · J. Taponen · J. Houtsonen (✉) · V. Huotari
Police University College, Tampere, Finland
e-mail: jarmo.houtsonen@polamk.fi

© The Author(s) 2018
G. Leventakis, M. R. Haberfeld (eds.), *Societal Implications of Community-Oriented Policing and Technology*, SpringerBriefs in Criminology,
https://doi.org/10.1007/978-3-319-89297-9_2

thinking can be deployed for improving CP services. Next we introduce a concrete tool for the police in building strategic partnerships: a Service Design Canvas for Community Policing that was applied in the Unity project financed by European Commission from its Horizon2020 program during a Finnish pilot exercise.[1]

Community Policing and Aspects of Strategy

Strategy is regarded useful for CP in three related senses of the term. At the most fundamental level CP needs strategy to reflect its overall purpose. Next, strategy helps to depict feasible journeys from the present situation to the desired future. In CP with multiple focus groups and partnerships a whole number of strategic purposes is likely to come up. A challenge is how to make the purposes meet in a fruitful way. Strategy assists in addressing various security issues that concern different communities and collaborative partners. Consequently, CP service design should not be police-centric but interactive. It should be based on information of the various security needs and utilize the analysis of the underlying mechanisms behind the security issues (see Pawson and Tilley 1997). Furthermore, CP should engage partners to search sustainable solutions for these issues.

CP as a specific way of policing is as much a strategic question as it is tactical and operational task. Strategic design of CP should start from critical analysis of the current position, and the available resources and capabilities, thus helping to make most out of the circumstances. Authorities, such as the police, often understand their purpose rather strictly as something statutory. On the other hand, police is also agile to borrow the latest business management vocabulary, such as being customer oriented, while at the same time resisting, contesting or decoupling any substantive changes in work processes and the scope of tasks (Goodson and Lindblad 2011). Fulfilling the strategic purpose presupposes critical revision of both processes and tasks. This includes a reflection of professional mandates and jurisdictions, and a possibility to re-distribute tasks between other professions or occupations. Often security issues are more than police matters and the analysis of underlying mechanisms may reveal a need for collaborative intervention.

Favoreu et al. (2016) divide three different aspects in the strategy formulation process: rational, political and collaborative. These aspects don't refute each other but vary at different phases of strategy process. Rational approach to strategy emphasizes the effective alignment of goals, targets and means, and suggests that activities are organized and led on the basis of valid situation picture. Political approach points out various interests that individuals and groups carry to strategic planning. In CP *collaborative aspect* underlies strategy process, which is an opportunity to improve interaction and mutual learning among stakeholders. (see Favoreu et al. 2016).

---

[1]This paper is based on pilot testing in Finland done within the Unity project funded by the European Commission within the H2020 Framework Programme (Grant Agreement: 653729).

Unity as a Community Policing Research and Innovation Project

The fundamental vision of the Unity project was to strengthen the connection between the police and stakeholders to improve the safety and security of communities and citizens. Unity wanted to develop CP concept that is flexible and adaptable to local contexts around Europe. The general idea of CP had to be adjusted to multiple conditions where Unity project conducted pilot testing of its products.[2] This adaptation required strategic analysis of the current conditions, the needs of the police forces and the communities, and the resources available for the common journey to the desired future. This exercise can utilize widely tested instruments, such as SWOT or PESTEL analysis. The same analytic tools can also be applied on a smaller scale for solving particular security problems undermining the livelihood of communities and the well-being of citizens.

Based on a large survey among the LEAs and stakeholders in eight European countries the Unity project set its goal to improve CP in six outcome areas: (1) trust and confidence, (2) accountability, (3) information sharing and communication, (4) addressing local needs, (5) collaborative problem solving, and (6) crime prevention (proactive policing). Unity project aimed to improve CP in these outcome areas in each pilot context. Important aspect of piloting was also the testing of how Unity technology would help CP processes to create value in the above-mentioned outcome areas.

Strategy Put into Practice – A Case of Puhos Shopping Center in Helsinki

One of the Unity pilot cases in Finland was the safety and security situation at an old shopping center in Helsinki. Puhos shopping center is located in a suburb nearby much larger and more modern shopping mall accessed easily by public transportation. When Puhos was opened in 1965, it was the largest of its kind in Finland. Today the old section seems almost empty while most of the business and other activities are in the new section. Enterprises, except for bars, started to move to the modern shopping mall, leaving several business spaces unoccupied. The plot is held by the municipality, but the real estate company is possessed by small-scale owners who have approximately 25% of shares, of whom a substantial proportion are immigrants, and large corporations who have about 75% of shares. The property is badly deteriorated and needs urgent renovation. Herein things become complicated, because, first, small-scale owners are afraid that the costs of repair will be far too expensive. Second, small-scale owners are concerned that large corporate owners

---

[2] Besides Finland, the pilot exercise was run in Belgium, Bulgaria, Croatia, Estonia, Germany, Macedonia and the UK.

want to sell the real estate to someone who would pull it down and construct new buildings. Some of the small-scale owners have an idea of developing the company with some investors towards a multicultural shopping mall and service center. The municipality has announced that it won't renew the rental agreement as it ends in 2020; it plans to erect high rise residential area, apart from the old section that is architectural object of protection.

Little by little the open business offices have been acquired by ethnic restaurateurs and various service entrepreneurs and a Muslim prayer house. All these little changes have revitalized the center and gradually strengthened the sense of community and solidarity between entrepreneurs who offer provisions and other services particularly for ethnic customers. Along with the above, specialized social services for diverse groups, such as substance abusers, socially marginalized or isolated people, and immigrant youngsters, were established at the area or nearby by the municipality and non-governmental organizations.

In spring 2016 the police learned through the Somali community that the security situation at the Puhos mall was in decline. Drugs were used quite openly at the mall and the small forest area behind the mall was full of used syringes. Drug addicts peddled stolen goods in public and aggressive collection of drug debts was commonly seen. During the past few years, the area received also more and more vagrants from East Europe. Furthermore, a group of young immigrant men held the mall as their own "territory". They acted violently against white people, especially women. A closer inspection revealed that these young men had arrived in Finland during the early 1990s, after having been lived in the UK during the past decade. Their passports were expired and therefore they had to return to Finland where they did not have any apartments, relatives or other social contacts outside their immediate circle of friends. When running up against problems they did not dare to contact the police or other public authorities.

The prayer house or the mosque at the mall is the largest in the district. The staff does not want to get involved in the troubles outside although these tend to disturb the daily activities at the mosque. The members of the community also assume that talking to authorities would likely entail more nuisance and the security problems would fall upon the activities in the prayer rooms instead of staying outside. The community members tend not to trust the authorities or the impartiality and competence of the police to solve their security problems. Representatives of migrant community have seen that the first challenge is the assumption that the municipality does not value the area and wants to pull it down. Due to the uncertainty of the continuity people are not well motivated to look after and clean the common premises. The second challenge is that many individuals, who loiter there, need support to get back into society, but don't receive the services they need.

Community Policing in Puhos

Complex security problems such as the case of Puhos Shopping Center belong to the sphere of activity of the Preventative Policing Unit (PPU) at the Helsinki Police Department. The Unit was established in 2012 as a part of a large organizational reform. The main goal of the PPU is to enhance security in the city of Helsinki: early prevention of phenomena that pose a threat to the security of neighborhoods and the building of partnerships with various stakeholders. In practice this means cooperation with a multitude of actors, such as other local and national police units, public agencies, non-governmental organizations, civic associations and citizens of Helsinki. An essential aspect of the PPU's work is to build and maintain trust among all stakeholders and collectively try to solve possible security challenges. The basic working method is a refined version of problem oriented policing. All teams focus on those security threatening phenomena that require more thorough investigations into the root of the problems, which may not be possible by the more traditional law enforcement methods. By means of local problem solving methods teams try to identify the factors behind crimes and disorder and then move on to influence those circumstances in collaboration with other police units, public agencies, NGOs and residents.

The Puhos case involves agents from both public and private sector and civil society. Therefore the case is difficult for the police to manage. A prerequisite for solving the problems is bringing all relevant stakeholders together and engaging them in improving the security and vitality of the area and its surroundings. Due to the large number of participants the arrangement of meetings and agreeing on schedules and agenda is very challenging. Police would also need to carefully identify the best channels to reach different community groups and stakeholders. For the present, police have communicated with phones and emails, as there is no common digital platform that could be used for exchanging information, booking meetings, or archiving documents. Activities and documents are difficult to manage, because there are so many agencies involved and the problems comprise a complex and intertwined totality. Often half of the major stakeholders have been left out from the meetings; a fact that has increased suspicion among the absentees.

A fundamental challenge has been that there is a lack of shared strategy and prioritization of issues. It has not been clear which agency is in the best position to lead the problem solving process of each individual case. Shared vision and well-defined, likely solvable security challenges can function as motivators that may help bring various agents together on a more permanent basis. In an ideal situation all agencies could have a voice in identifying and prioritizing security issues, exchanging information and experimenting with alternative solutions. Concrete cooperation would improve communication, trust and commitment to seek more sustainable solutions.

The current state of affairs should be improved at least in two respects. First, the problem solving process should be designed to be more systematic, inventive and effective. This requires, for instance, agreed rules for organizing meetings, allocating tasks, identifying, analyzing and prioritizing security issues, constructing, testing and evaluating solutions. Second, the problem solving process should be supported by a Collaborative Problems Solving Platform (CPSP), a digital tool and a virtual meeting place to share information, discuss and debate, archive documents, and allow relevant agencies to participate. Platform should help the process management and enable evaluation of impact of activities. This type of platform, including an app and an analytic engine, was developed and piloted within the Unity -project. Although it is a prototype in the making, it was warmly welcomed by the end-users, the police and the other agencies in Helsinki.

Service Design Canvas for Community Policing

During the Unity project, team at the Police University College (Finland) developed on the basis of business model canvas a strategy tool named a Service Design Canvas for Community Policing (SDCCP).[3] The tool is for addressing and prioritizing the needs of communities and citizens, setting goals while recognizing how various resources, activities, partners and channels may have an effect on the outcomes. Service Design can be used as an overall strategy tool, or as a more specified tool that suggests actions or programs to solve the individual problems identified by the SWOT analysis or by some other means. In the case of Puhos, this tool was used e.g. to find the added value of CP and to identify the key partners and channels of communication.

There are nine elements in the SDCCP template. It can be filled by the police or, preferably in collaboration with the community partners, as was the case in Puhos. The first five elements are about the operational environment of CP. At the beginning, the participants should define who are the *Key Customers of CP*? Which communities, individuals, or neighborhoods will be the key beneficiaries? To whom CP is creating value through solving security problems and increasing safety? This requires thorough discussion and judgement, because customers are known by their problems, but not all problems are police issues.

Next phase requires imagination and innovation. The participants of the local problem solving process, that is, the police and stakeholders alike, should put forward a *Unique Value Proposition* of CP. What kind of added value are CP activities providing for the communities, neighborhoods or particular individuals? What kind of security or safety needs and expectations should CP meet? The proposed solutions or programs should be accepted by the community, neighborhoods or citizens who will be the recipients of the services. Therefore, it is important that they are also given a voice, directly or indirectly, in the service design process. The third element in the SDCCP is the identification of the main *Communication and Contacting Channels* with the Key Customers. Through which channels do

---

[3] The original business model canvas is distributed under a Creative Commons license from Strategyzer AG and can be used without any restrictions for modeling businesses.

community members want to be reached? Channels could be various types of ICT tools, such as platforms usable by PCs or smartphones, but also the more traditional arenas, such as community meetings and the use of trusted intermediaries. It is useful to consider pros and cons of the ways and tools that are used currently for approaching various community members and individuals. Additionally, one should review how various channels are or could be integrated together, e.g. will there be a joint platform for email, social media and the Internet? Which channels have worked well so far or would likely work in the future? It is also important to consider the aspects of security and cost-efficiency of various options if digital services will be considered for communication and repository.

Fourthly, the users of the service design canvas should analyze the quality and intensity of all significant *Customer Relationships*. Several questions are relevant here. How would you describe the relationships with the relevant community partners? How would you like to change these relations? How strong is the level of trust between different parties in the collaborative problem solving network? What is the intensity and quality of collaboration and communication between the parties? How well are the police and its practices accepted by different community members? Are the police officers able to reach all the key communities, especially minorities and groups or individuals in a marginal or weak position? Why are some individuals difficult to reach? The final element of the operational environment is the evaluation of *Societal Impact* of the problem and the benefits that will be received from its successful resolution. The point of departure is the breaking down of the level of crime and disorder within the community. Who are the perpetrators, victims and third parties? How do the citizens perceive the situation, how subjective perceptions of security are related to objective facts? Do the local community partners feel a sense of empowerment and ownership when they can contribute to the problem solving efforts? How do the police officers feel about their work and working conditions? What is the quantity and quality of information and to what extent it is shared between the parties?

After recognizing the needs for security and well-being, one is ready to start designing an operational CP model. This comprises of defining the *kKey aActivities*, *Key Resources* and *Strategic Partners* and finally making a *Cost Structure* assessment. The sixth phase is to define the Key Activities in CP at large or in relation to individual security issue. What kind of operational policing do the value propositions require? In other words, what needs to be done and how? The next step is defining the Key Resources available for CP. What human, technological, organizational, economic, administrative and legal resources are needed? Resources can include various competencies: skills, knowledge and motivation needed to work for the service of the community. The eighth element is about looking back the Key Communities and considering, who are the key partners of CP in general, or in solving some single issues? Who can help in delivering CP services and finding solutions to problems? Which key resources these partners can bring with them for the benefit of the whole network? Which Key Activities could the partners perform? What would be their specific roles and responsibilities in the collaboration? The final element in the canvas service design is the analysis of the Cost Structure of CP with the defined resources, partnerships and activities. How much do alternative resources, activities and communication channels cost? One should compare the cost efficiency of current CP and the planned working model. Costs and benefits can also be calculated for various kinds of solutions.

The ultimate goal in using the SDCCP is developing value for and with the customers, or rather the partners of the police. The strong point of the tool is that it can be outlined on one page. It can be completed together with stakeholders, and if necessary, be tested and assessed with another group to gain more validity. The feedback from stakeholders and the community members can help assess whether the chosen CP service design strategy is desirable. The first few CP interventions may be not be perfect, but it is important that stakeholders tolerate some chaos and allow collaborative learning.

Conclusions

Because at the core of CP is the collaboration between partners to prevent crime and disorder, and thereby to improve the quality of life and well-being, a wide representative of stakeholders and citizens are invited to co-create solutions. Moreover, CP is a slow-burn service-oriented style of policing, instead of reactive and control oriented style of law enforcement (Clamp and Paterson 2017). Rather than engaging solely in continuous improvement of their own work, the police should become more adept at sharing experiences and lay knowledge with partners. Bueermann (2012, 19) predicts that in the future police will be more and more a broker and a facilitator for community action to solve problems related to crime and disorder. The role of citizens and civic associations will change from mere consumers to partners and co-producers who will add their local knowledge, skills and resources to the production of security services. As security becomes public good that is co-produced through various networks and actors, the police should increase their understanding of the joint processes this involves. This article aimed at offering such understanding by discussing about perspectives and tools for improving CP services. More specifically, the paper described one practical tool: Service Design Canvas for Community Policing, which could be advantageous for constructing the overall strategy for community police, or just trying to collaboratively solve local security issues with the communities and citizens.

References

Bueermann, J. (2012). Preparing the police for an uncertain future: Four guiding principles. In D. R. Cohen McCullough & D. L. Spence (Eds.), *American policing in. 2022: Essays on the Future of a Profession. COPS, U.S. Department of Justice.* http://ric-zai-inc.com/Publications/cops-p235-pub.pdf. Accessed 23 Nov 2017.

Clamp, K., & Paterson, C. (2017). *Restorative policing. Concepts, theory and practice*. Abingdon: Routledge.

Den Boer, M. (2014). Intelligence-led policing in Europe. Lingering between idea and implementation. In I. Duyvesteyn, B. de Jong, & J. van Reijn (Eds.), *The future of intelligence: Challenges in the 21st century*. London: Routledge.

Favoreu, C. D., Carassus, D., & Maurel, C. (2016). Strategic management in the public sector: A rational, political or collaborative approach? *International Review of Administrative Sciences, 82*(3), 435–453. https://doi.org/10.1177/0020852315578410.

Frevel, B., & Rogers, C. (2016). Community partnerships (UK) vs Crime Prevention Councils (GER): Differences and similarities. *Police Journal: Theory, Practice and Principle., 89*(2), 133–150. https://doi.org/10.1177/0032258X16641426.

Fyfe, N., Terpstra, J., & Tops, P. (2013). *Centralizing forces? Comparative perspectives on contemporary police reforms in northern and Western Europe*. Hague: Eleven.

Goodson, I. F., & Lindblad, S. (2011). Conclusions: Developing a conceptual framework for understanding professional knowledge. In I. F. Goodson & S. Lindblad (Eds.), *Professional knowledge and educational restructuring in Europe*. Rotterdam: Sense Publishers.

Hoogenboom, B. (2010). *The governance of policing and security – Ironies, myths and paradoxes*. Basingstoke: Palgrave MacMillan.

Pawson, R., & Tilley, N. (1997). *Realistic evaluation*. London: Sage.

Shearing, C., & Johnston, L. (2010). Nodal wars and network fallacies. *Theoretical Criminology, 14*(4), 1362–4806.

White, A. (2011). The new political economy of private security. *Theoretical Criminology, 16*(1), 85–101. https://doi.org/10.1177/1362480611410903.

Open Access This chapter is licensed under the terms of the Creative Commons Attribution 4.0 International License (http://creativecommons.org/licenses/by/4.0/), which permits use, sharing, adaptation, distribution and reproduction in any medium or format, as long as you give appropriate credit to the original author(s) and the source, provide a link to the Creative Commons license and indicate if changes were made.

The images or other third party material in this chapter are included in the chapter's Creative Commons license, unless indicated otherwise in a credit line to the material. If material is not included in the chapter's Creative Commons license and your intended use is not permitted by statutory regulation or exceeds the permitted use, you will need to obtain permission directly from the copyright holder.

Chapter 3
Crowd Knowledge Sourcing – A Potential Methodology to Uncover Victims of Human Trafficking

Julia Muraszkiewicz

Introduction

Gary Marx wrote that 'Whether dealing with questions of justice, quality of life, security, health, the environment or other issues, the potential benefits of science and technology are hardly deniable'(Marx 2012).Yet, at the same time he is a profound champion of caution when it comes to technology. In 1985 Melvin Kranzberg, a historian of technology, delivered the address at the annual meeting of the Society for the History of Technology, in which he presented what is already known as Kranzberg's six laws of technology (Sacasas 2011). The first and most insightful one is that "Technology is neither good nor bad; nor is it neutral." Thus, the notion of technology always needs to be justified, controlled and should serve a purpose and not just be developed for the sake of it. This ethos forms the critical lens through which a recent use of technology by Europol is scrutinised in this article.

Today, technology provides opportunities to enable the participation of citizens and communities in policing at their chosen level (Longstaff et al. 2015, p.38). Simultaneously technology allows law enforcement agencies (LEAs) to better harness the knowledge possessed by communities and use local intelligence to address crimes. This is especially true of crimes that happen in the community, one such crime is the exploitation of persons e.g., through human trafficking. This can be achieved through the use of crowd knowledge sourcing solutions (defined below).

In July 2017, the BBC published an article detailing how Europe's police agency, Europol, has launched a webpage displaying images from instances of child sex abuse in an attempt to find the perpetrators and victims by asking members of society to report details that may point to intelligence. Europol's initiative provides a welcome opportunity to reflect on the opportunities brought about by technology in

J. Muraszkiewicz (✉)
Trilateral Research Ltd, London, UK
e-mail: julia.muraszkiewicz@trilateralresearch.com

© The Author(s) 2018
G. Leventakis, M. R. Haberfeld (eds.), *Societal Implications of Community-Oriented Policing and Technology*, SpringerBriefs in Criminology,
https://doi.org/10.1007/978-3-319-89297-9_3

the fight against a crime such as human trafficking. However, this author, even in her role as a promoter of the use of technology in addressing hidden and complex crimes, has to recognise the limits. The chapter thus aims to stand alongside others (Gerry et al. 2016) as part of an on-going and comprehensive debate on the role of technology in fighting human trafficking. It will be argued that whilst using crowd knowledge sourcing is an interesting method of harnessing aggregate knowledge amassed by society it is still a difficult and learning process, and may require better broadcasting.

Crowd Knowledge Sourcing: Explained and Exemplified

Crowd Sourcing is the utilization of the knowledge possessed by Web users for the collection and/or analysis of mass data (Howe 2006). Milo emphasizes that *Wikipedia* 'is probably the earliest and best known example of crowd-sourced data and an illustration of what can be achieved with a crowd-based data sourcing model'(Milo 2011). *Crowd Knowledge Sourcing* is conceptualized in this chapter as Crowd Sourcing that relies on harnessing people's knowledge. It is rooted in the reality that knowledge and data is embedded in society; we are a knowledge society.

One of the advantages of crowd sourcing is that anyone can contribute. Thus, those using it (in this case LEAs) have access to a wider knowledge pool. Crowd Knowledge Sourcing is enabled by the Internet and Web 2.0 technologies and 'In the Internet era, this has a great potential of generating information repositories that are otherwise very difficult to construct and for identifying new unforeseen solutions and products. The potential for cost-savings associated with crowd data sourcing also provides attractive procurement alternatives to companies bound to tight budgets, particularly during economic downturns' (Milo 2011).

The inherent characteristic of any crowd sourcing is that it relies entirely on participants making a voluntary contribution; in other words there is no contract, no salary and no obligation. Participants may decide which tasks to undertake, when and how much time they dedicate. Moreover, their work is not the product of market forces or any hierarchies (Wittke and Hanekop 2011, p.9), which undeniably means that participants 'are not subject to [...] instructions or assignment of tasks, nor are they under any obligation to perform or provide a particular service' (Wittke and Hanekop 2011, p.12).

Despite the fact that crowd sourcing relies on voluntary participation, large numbers of society members contribute; cases such as Wikipedia or open source software stand as proof. As concluded by Wittke and Hanekop (2011, p.12): 'voluntary contributions here are not on a small scale, nor sporadic or exceptional, but on a very large scale, systematic, and with lasting returns.' The key to success however is predominantly reliant on the task in question appealing to a large number of persons; whether because it is enjoyable, interesting, glorifying, gratifying or allows self-development and the establishment of a respectable online profile. Furthermore, von Hippel (2005, p.5) explains that persons will engage in crowd sourcing type activates if they result will benefit them directly. This can be justified by the references to rational choice theories. Importantly for this paper, this explanation for the success of crowd-sourced initiatives may cause an issue when we aim to rely on the community to fight human trafficking. This will be explained below, however in brief it is hypothesized that because the time and effort put in, is not toward one's own use or direct and obvious benefit, challenges as to efficiency will arise.

Proposals to Use Crowd Knowledge Sourcing to Rescue Victims of Human Trafficking and Bring Perpetrators to Justice

An array of factors contribute to the crime of human trafficking and it is widely accepted that the crime is related 'to different fields and interests: migration, organized crime, prostitution, human right, violence against women, the feminization of poverty, the gender division of the international labour market, unequal international economic relationships, etc' (Wijers and Van Doorninck 2005). To that list we can add technology, including the Internet. In particular, the Internet assists in sexual exploitation for it provides a space for traffickers and other exploiters to engage in illegal activities. Posting pictures of victims – whether to advertise their services or as part of online pornography – allows perpetrators to span across borders and reach unprecedented level of audiences. It also provides a cloak of invisibility; it is harder to find someone posting images from their bedroom then to spot a brothel in a city. This adds to trafficking as a prominent and complex security issue.

Tackling this phenomenon unsurprisingly requires new savvy resources; this is because the hidden and evolving nature of the crime mean that there is a natural limit to what law enforcements authorities will be able to do. As aptly highlighted by Couch (2016): '[h]uman trafficking cases can live or die based on how quickly detectives gather evidence. Several emerging technologies aim to speed up that process, including Traffic Jam, a software program launched in 2013 that combs through escort ads and uses machine learning to find patterns that can connect ads across multiple geographic locations to the same organization or pimp.' Technology thus provides LEAs with a new variation of gathering intelligence.

Detection of content that potentially concerns exploited persons is now common practice; 'software such as PhotoDNA can automatically detect illicit content' (Drewer and Ellermann 2016, p.200). The harder part can be determining where the victims who feature in the images or videos are being harboured and exploited. The police can take the content off line, but how, using the existing images, can they get access to the victims and help them? On balance the analysis of images – studying them and trying to uncover potential clues as to the whereabouts of the actors concerned – is an enormous task. This task can potentially be eased through the use of Crowd Knowledge Sourcing tools as recently demonstrated by Europol. In the on-going search for how to solve missing pieces of a crime puzzle and related to this, recognising their own limits, Europol launched a Crowd Knowledge Sourcing website: https://www.europol.europa.eu/stopchildabuse.

Criminals exploit human beings in a space that can be filled with clues as to their whereabouts. These clues are of course discrete, unrecognisable by most. However, in all likelihood there are persons in our society who will be able to identify a logo on a shopping bag in the corner of a room and connect it to a local shop. Or, they may spot packaging from a local takeaway and tell the Police which neighbourhood the exploitation has taken place.

The Europol site displays parts of images connected to child sex abuse, i.e. only showing one object. As summarised by Europol: 'The objects are all taken from the background of an image with sexually explicit material involving minors. For all images below, every other investigative avenue has already been examined. Therefore we are requesting your assistance in identifying the origin of some of these objects. We are convinced that more eyes will lead to more leads and will ultimately help to save these children.' The website showcases new approaches to how the police can access information with regards to cases of exploitation, which take place on the Internet. Whilst Europol is using the site for cases of sexual abuse concerning minors, the methodology can be extended to online cases of human trafficking.

An analysis of clues contained in images is potentially a good use of Crowd Knowledge Sourcing. In simplest terms it aims to rely on the public to help collect and figure out pieces of a crime jigsaw. To that end a number of images are uploaded, and 'each photo has an option underneath to send an anonymous tip to Europol or share on social media. The detectives want users to realise the potentially vital role they can play, they believe a few clicks could help to rescue a child' (BBC 2017). The Europol tool could potentially be a powerful mechanism by which communication on investigations is eased, moreover it can also have a significant impacts on public perceptions of the police: they are seen to be working hard at solving a heinous crime.

Challenges of Using Crowd Knowledge Sourcing and Recommendations for the Way Forward

Whilst the opportunities seem advantageous, questions arise about the likelihood of success and benefit. Building upon insights from Gary Marx we must acknowledge however that no matter how 'ideal a technical control system may appear in the abstract under ideal laboratory conditions or successful in the short run, the world of application is often much messier and more complicated than the public relations efforts claim' (Marx 2012). Marx understands that there is rarely a perfect technical solution, or one without issues. The same is true of a technical answer to community problems.

In an attempt to challenge emerging technologies, scholars may first look to the privacy and ethical implications, particular when it comes to the domain of law enforcement technology. As highlighted by Finn et al. 'privacy is a key lens though which many new technologies, and most especially new surveillance technologies, are critiqued' (Finn et al. 2013, p.4). In the instance of the Europol platform however, it would seem that the identity of the victims and potential perpetrators is safeguarded through the method of removing any identifiable images. The removing of potentially sensitive data and anonymization of the images is a welcome step from the perspective of privacy law as well as ethics. Drewer and Ellermann (2016, p.197) writing about the European Counter Terrorism Centre highlight that 'the balance between privacy and security has always been central to law enforcement operations. Europol is proud to have implemented one of the most robust data protection regimes in the world of law enforcement. This allows the organisation to effectively support and strengthen Member States action in preventing and combating serious crime while duly respecting individuals' right for privacy.' There seems to be no deviation from this in using Crowd Knowledge Sourcing. The pictures show the bare minimum, and there are no personal sensitive data visible. Thus, the values around the human right to privacy, supposedly, remain intact.

Notwithstanding the above commendation for the Europol solution, it is suggested that our enthusiasm for the technology can be curbed by practical restrains; namely the requirement for an active, willing and diverse public. It is suggested that it is likely that interaction with a system like the one offered by Europol will be limited to those *in the know* of the system. Moreover, those in the know (e.g., relevant stakeholders working in this field) may not be the type of audience best matched for analysing the images. A successful identification relies on someone spotting a piece of local knowledge, and thus it requires the use of every day citizens across the relevant geographic space (e.g., the EU). To ensure accuracy and reliability law enforcement actors need to engage with the community at large. The likelihood, although the author found no available data as to the exact figures, is that the number of those in the know of the platform is relatively low compared to what would be required for wide-scale success. If society is not aware of the platform it logically follows that they will not use it. One recommendation that arises therefore is to better communicate the existence of the Crowd Knowledge Sourcing platform so as to ensure an inflow of participation from the general public. This, to a certain extent is being done as evidenced by the above-mentioned BBC article and also social media campaigns. However, ensuring the engagement of the community also requires support at not just neighbourhood levels but also at policy level; e.g., through the provision of funds to disseminate information about the various initiatives.

Related to the issue of ensuring a wide usage, is the question of motivation. What persuades large number of society members to regularly log on to the Europol system and examine the images? It is hypothesised that altruistic motivation would be the biggest factor, however this should be empirically researched. How much force does altruism carry? How can we increase the motivation? Myhill makes an interesting point with regard to community policing more generally that can be transferred to the case of Europol's platform. 'Communities may not initially have the willingness to engage with the police, particularly in areas where there is a history of poor relations. This can sometimes be interpreted by officers as apathy. The police need to foster trust and confidence in these communities prior to attempting to secure community participation' (Myhill 2006, p.84). Thus what is needed is not only motivation, but also trust and confidence in the police and in their methods. This includes confidence that the platform is working. Myhill thus rightly highlights that 'the police must value the input and contribution of the public if partnerships are to be successful. Information flow must be two-way. The police need to provide communities with feedback on how their contribution is being used. If action is taken, this should be publicised. If action is not taken, the reasons for this should be explained' (Myhill 2006, p.85). Thus it is recommended that any initiative that seeks to rely on the society to help in solving crime puzzles also show cases the positive impact community involvement has had.

A further question arises, how can law enforcement authorities ensure that a momentum of motivation to voluntarily engage in this form of community participation is sustained? We can imagine that after seeing an advert about the Crowd Knowledge Sourcing site or reading about it on the news, individuals will log on. However, how do we make sure they regularly come back? Presumably much relates to socially embedding crowd knowledge sourcing in communities and again showing how their work is effective.

Concluding Remarks

This paper has reiterated the notion that human trafficking can be a hidden crime, difficult for law enforcement agencies to uncover and obtain evidence of. Yet the obligations on States stemming from international and regional legislation such as the 2011 EU Directive on Human Trafficking and policy requires due diligent crime investigation. Technological solutions are increasingly being proposed along with traditional approaches as a way to address crimes, including that of human trafficking and exploitation generally. Here there is potentially some room for Crowd Knowledge Sourcing as exemplified by Europol. Alongside introducing the technology this article sought to, through citing Gary Marx acknowledge that we should not blindly engage in a celebratory ethos of technology but approach it with scrutiny. We should question if it breaches the right to privacy and if it is in fact useful. As Marx says 'A police chief who says "if the technology is available, why not use it?" needs first to ask, "what are the likely consequences of using this technology, how does its use compare to that of other technologies and to the consequences of doing nothing?" (Marx 2003, p.25). It is argued by this author that the Europol online platform provides aggregate evidence gathering pathways, and opportunities to harness inherent knowledge held by the public that may otherwise not have reached the LEAs. It is a modus operandi that has been developed because all other options have been exhausted and the LEAs have reached a stalemate. However, to make the platform a successful instrument, we must address the important challenge of gathering crowd participation. The article recommends that two simultaneous approaches need to be undertaken. Firstly, there should be further research about what motivates persons to participate in community policing and how to ensure their engagement, specifically with regard to technology. Secondly, there should be greater efforts to communicate the existence of the tool, including from those at policy level. TV and radio ads are possible platforms. In addition, usage could be made of community clusters such as faith groups, which transcend socio-economic demographics.

References

BBC. (2017). Europol shows clues from child abuse images to track offenders. [Online] http://www.bbc.co.uk/news/world-europe-40115549

Couch, C. (2016). How artificial intelligence can stop sex trafficking. *PBS* [Online] http://www.pbs.org/wgbh/nova/next/tech/sex-trafficking/

Drewer, D., & Ellermann, J. (2016). May the (well-balanced) force be with us! The launch of the European Counter Terrorism Centre (ECTC). *Computer Law & Security Review: The International Journal of Technology Law and Practice, 32*, 195–204.

Europol. (n.d.). Stop child abuse – Trace an object. [Online] https://www.europol.europa.eu/stopchildabuse

Finn, R., Wright, D., & Friedewald, M. (2013). Seven types of privacy. In S. Gutwirth, R. Leenes, & P. De Hert (Eds.), *European data protection: Coming of age?* (pp. 3–32). Dordrecht: Springer.

Gerry, F., Muraszkiewicz, J., & Vavoula, N. (2016). The role of technology in the fight against human trafficking: Reflections on privacy and data protection concerns. *Computer Law and Security Review, 32*(2), 205–217.

Howe, J. (2006). The rise of crowdsourcing. *Wired Magazine* – Issue 14.06, [Online] https://www.wired.com/2006/06/crowds/

Longstaff, A., Willer, J., Chapman, J., Czarnosmki, S., & Graham, J. (2015). Neighbourhood policing: Past, present and future. *The Police Foundation*. [Online] http://www.police-foundation.org.uk/uploads/catalogerfiles/neighbourhood-policing-past-present-and-future---a-review-of-the-literature/neighbourhood_policing_past_present_future.pdf

Marx, G. (2003). Some information age techno-fallacies. *Journal of Contingencies and Crisis Management, 11*(1), 25–31.

Marx, G. (2012). Technology and social control: The search for the illusive silver bullet continues. *Encyclopedia of the Social & Behavioral Sciences, 2nd edition*, [Online] http://web.mit.edu/gtmarx/www/techsoccon.html

Milo, T. (2011). Crowd-based data sourcing. In S. Kikuchi et al. (Eds.), *7th international workshop of databases in networked information systems*. Heidelberg: Springer.

Myhill, A. (2006). Community engagement in policing Lessons from the literature. National Policing Improvement Agency. [Online] http://whatworks.college.police.uk/Research/Documents/Community_engagement_lessons.pdf

Sacasas, M. (2011). Kranzberg's six laws of technology, a metaphor, and a story. [Online] https://thefrailestthing.com/2011/08/25/kranzbergs-six-laws-of-technology-a-metaphor-and-a-story/

Von Hippel, E. (2005). *Democratizing innovation*. Cambridge: The MIT Press.

Wijers, M., & Van Doorninck, M. (2005). What's wrong with the anti-trafficking framework? *Background Paper For The European Conference On Sex Work, Human Rights, Labour And Migration. ICRSE (International Committee On The Rights Of Sex Workers In Europe).* [Online]. http://www.ide.go.jp/English/Publish/Download/Dp/pdf/289.pdf

Wittke, V., & Hanekop, H. (2011). New forms of collaborative innovation and production on the internet. In V. Wittke & H. Hanekop (Eds.), *New forms of collaborative innovation and production on the internet. An interdisciplinary perspective* (pp. 9–29). Universität Göttingen: Göttingen.

Open Access This chapter is licensed under the terms of the Creative Commons Attribution 4.0 International License (http://creativecommons.org/licenses/by/4.0/), which permits use, sharing, adaptation, distribution and reproduction in any medium or format, as long as you give appropriate credit to the original author(s) and the source, provide a link to the Creative Commons license and indicate if changes were made.

The images or other third party material in this chapter are included in the chapter's Creative Commons license, unless indicated otherwise in a credit line to the material. If material is not included in the chapter's Creative Commons license and your intended use is not permitted by statutory regulation or exceeds the permitted use, you will need to obtain permission directly from the copyright holder.

Chapter 4
Addressing Ethical Challenges of Creating New Technology for Criminal Investigation: The VALCRI Project

P. Duquenoy, D. Gotterbarn, K. K. Kimppa, N. Patrignani, and B. L. William Wong

Introduction

For the past 3 years, we have been working on a European Union project involving multiple partnerships between software developers and several EU police departments to develop a decision support system based on ground-breaking technology. Three key problems identified and to be addressed by the project, were (DoW 2014, pp. 5–6): (a) Problems of interacting with a large dataset in Intelligence Analysis – processing large amounts of data into actionable intelligence; (b) Problems in Information Analysis facing the Analyst – making sense of large volumes of data, assembling relevant information in meaningful ways; (c) Problems arising from the Lack of Technical Skills – need user-interface that works with, and for analysts. To overcome these challenges the project aims to support intelligence analysis by providing "a system that facilitates human reasoning and analytic discourse, tightly coupled with semi-automated human-mediated semantic knowledge extraction." (http://valcri.org/). To avoid any potential ethical, social or privacy concerns this project was reviewed by an independent ethics board and guided by an internal Legal, Ethics and Privacy group (LEP).

P. Duquenoy (✉) · B. L. William Wong
Middlesex University, London, UK

D. Gotterbarn
Software Engineering Ethics Research Institute, Department of Computing,
East Tennessee State University, Johnson City, Tennessee, USA
e-mail: don@gotterbarn.com

K. K. Kimppa
University of Turku, Turku, Finland

N. Patrignani
Universita Cattolicà del Sacro Cuore, Milan, Italy

© The Author(s) 2018
G. Leventakis, M. R. Haberfeld (eds.), *Societal Implications of Community-Oriented Policing and Technology*, SpringerBriefs in Criminology,
https://doi.org/10.1007/978-3-319-89297-9_4

VALCRI Explained

The goals of the project are to: (a) "Assist police in the analysis of large and complex datasets in support of intelligence and investigative work; (b) Facilitate human reasoning and analytic discourse; (c) Augment rather than replace human decision-making; (d) Protect against human cognitive bias and abuses arising from accidental, inadvertent or deliberate violations of ethical, legal and privacy principles." (Shepherd 2015). The technical objectives of the project included developing: a system that addresses bias mitigation, social and legal factors into a single principled framework that developers can use to guide the system design. (DoW, pp. 9–10). The development team was skilled in solving the technical problems, but there were a host of other issues to address: legal constraints about ".privacy and security, and some significant ethical issues. Addressing the ethical and social constraints during development required an interactive process where the project could regularly be reviewed. To do this the project brought together technical designers, ethics, law and privacy experts, several end-user groups from EU as partners, and an independent ethics board. The main risks identified by the IEB were: Diverse social, professional and legal mores, privacy and data protection risks, risks of poor communication, data and reasoning provenance and the transparency of the entire analysis process for addressing significant ethical concerns. Issues related to cognitive bias were noted early in the project and mitigation measures in the form of design guidelines produced as part of the Human Issues Framework in WP3 (Haider et al. 2015).

Addressing Ethics in VALCRI

In the first stage ethics specialists were invited as members of an Independent Ethics Board (IEB) (composed of experienced ethics advisers) that would review and guide the project process from the ethics perspective, and ethics was specifically included in a work package (WP3) with the topics of privacy and law. During the project the legal, ethics, privacy group (LEP) was extended to include security (SEPL) to improve communications between the human issues side and the technical side, enabling the principles from LEP to be operationalised technically. To address both intentional and unintentional ethical lapses, the VALCRI project assigned the task of proactively identifying and developing ethical safeguards to the SEPL group and IEB. The concerns were with both process (alert developers to potential risk facilitated by their development of the software) and product (is the product ethically viable and does it mitigate known ethical problems). The teams identified modifications to the design and development which could be addressed by the system developers. Addressing these identified elements required ethical design beyond mere technological solutions. The built-in ethical safeguards were needed to have the system both identify and either prevent or alert individuals to alter their (unintentional) decision strategies.

Security, Ethics, Privacy and Legal Group (SEPL)

SEPL's task of communicating security, ethics, privacy, legal issues required the 'translation' of human factors requirements into language more relevant to the technical teams. The insights about the human factors problems from both IEB and SEPL will contribute to other research projects beyond the area of crime visualization, and also contribute to resolving a wider range of concerns present in other sensitive projects, such as concerns regarding logging the users' actions and documenting the reasoning processes for auditing and evidence (meeting the "Transparency in analysis" requirement mentioned earlier).

Communications Problems in a Multi-Tiered Approach

Systems development communications was a problem between teams and with the IEB. The SEPL group works well enough but unfortunately not all developers have representatives in this group creating difficulties in ensuring that the proposals for securing ethical resolutions have been communicated to implementers. Security, being a well-defined subject, became the primary focus of the group which resulted in mistakenly equating security and ethics. An unintended consequence of this arrangement was that teams initially reduced ethical issues to privacy and data security. The word 'security', when applied to "secure the rights of those stakeholders impacted by the system", was planned to be addressed by simply limiting access to the system, that is, data security. Initially privacy rights or securing rights not to be falsely accused (due to confirmation bias) were not included in the system.

Addressing IEB, SEPL, VALCRI Team Interactions

An early underlying issue was that the complexity and inter-relatedness of multiple IEB issues were not recognised. In order to keep track of the concerns that were raised by the IEB, and to make sure there was follow-up with the relevant technical groups, a spreadsheet listing the concerns was developed by management. This tool which could have been used to help communication between teams was used primarily as a task assignment device. For each concern on a row, a person or a group would be asked "How do you address this?" drawing responses like "It is not in the scope of our assignment" or "It is handled in the X module?" Since there was no management overview of the document, teams would have a different understanding of a concept or term depending on what function they were working on. What was meant by "track changes", "data reliability", and "transparency"? The way the concerns spreadsheet was used contributed to contradictory responses for issues about provenance. There was also a basic translation problem requiring technical people to interpret abstract issues raised by the IEB. What does "data transparency" actually mean to the different parties? These examples illustrate the significant limitations of document-based approaches to bridge the translation gap compared to face to face discussions. The benefits of the spreadsheet are recording and management of issues in one document (dates, notes added, a column for actions etc.) with the document providing a dynamic and ongoing record. The disadvantages are (i) sharing revisions with the IEB (ii) The nature of the document and the process (to contact relevant people in the consortium to ask if the issue is addressed) forces a 'silo' approach – that is a response to a specific issue and no other issues (iii) the issue can be phrased ambiguously (e.g. the 'transparency' example above) and responding to the concern as expressed in the document results in a query. Without face-to-face, or vocal communication in some way (that allows for queries, elaboration, explanations) the concerns expressed have to be interpreted by the responder who is mostly operating in unfamiliar territory – ethical/privacy/legal issues. If misinterpreted the responses are not likely to answer the concern. Both of these methods have benefits and both have been used, they are excellent methods for exploring the issues and sharing with developers the reasons why a particular item is an ethical concern. However, in the context of the 'face-to-face' option, unless someone has been allocated to record the detail, or some pre-prepared 'check sheet' is completed, records of the meeting rely on notes and remembering conversations.

Risks Identified

Some of the challenges faced and trade-offs required in developing and using a semi-automatic decision support system based on visually-aided thinking present different risks.

Standard risks There are different kinds of software risks; some are ethical risks discussed on the following pages, while others are common to most software projects. Initially, some risks such as changing legal constraints were not anticipated, including problems such as how to comply with the "right-to-an-explanation" feature of the new EU Data Protection (http://ec.europa.eu/justice/data-protection/). This requires "algorithm transparency" and "reasoning transparency". The systems development difficulty is that changes are required to provide both while also protecting classified policing techniques. Transparency as a concept applied to the project has been useful in alleviating some of the issues, for example, showing the user how the system is working, as well as making transparent user actions in allowing users to record their analysis process and sources of information on a particular case (Islam et al. 2017). In addition, the security protocols for the project include transparency in the capability to record access to the system, changes to policies of access, and readable (auditable) logs, and 'super-logs' accessible only by independent authorities (as described by Schlehahn et al. 2017). The point of this is that some of the ethical concerns have been addressed by the application of different technologies that have been organised into different domain types with the project, such as 'security', provenance, etc.

Ethical Social and Legal Risks due to the nature of the project IEB identified issues include: accidental discrimination, the Mosaic effect, algorithmic opacity, data aggregation with mixed levels of reliability, data and reasoning provenance, and various biases, (IEB 2017). Several of these issues were then addressed by white papers. VALCRI also tracked and evaluated these concerns by constructing scenarios in which the concern might arise, comparing it to current police practices, using standard technical risk approaches of estimating the probability, the significance of impact and considering mitigation strategies. The results of this work were then incorporated into the requirements and design. The thawing and refreezing of requirements leads to its own set of problems, discussed below. Amongst the difficulties identified are two closely related issues whose relation may not immediately be apparent; first, the fact that decision support is automated leads to overconfidence in the "computerized" results (Chen and Koufas 2015) and second, the use of visual thinking techniques encouraging intuitive insightful analysis which impacts the investigators obligation to produce 'communicable knowledge' which can be used by other investigators and can be used in courts. Techniques used to address this overconfidence tendency include recording the competence level of the analysts and each step in the analysis. But this left open issues of information bias – a tendency to ignore disconfirming instances. A system needs to make clear when the evidence for suggested possible relations displayed by it is weak. Showing multiple relationships as if they are all based on the same level of evidence opens the door to information bias which is more likely when predictions are vague and outcome feedback is ambiguous. This leads to an erroneous level of analyst confidence in weak decisions. On the other hand, other research indicates that our optimism about using skill level indicators for the analyst would not resolve the overconfidence problem. Research has shown that when a decision maker's experience level is low that they base their decision on the empirical data (explicit information), whereas those with a high or medium experience level focus on their previous experiences (implicit information) and have a tendency to ignore disconfirming evidence. Using skill levels as criteria may encourage later analysts to suffer from overconfidence bias. (Millitello 2017). Investigators also have an obligation to produce 'communicable knowledge' useable by other investigators and useable in courts. Resolving this problem helps to reduce overconfidence bias. To address this communicable knowledge concern requires the system to support transparently handling chains of reasoning – recording the reasons for decisions and connections made by the investigator, the articulation of the reasons by the investigator help develop communicable knowledge. Besides resolving the communicable knowledge concern, this approach addresses both the overconfidence in computerized decisions and the not looking at the empirical evidence overconfidence issue. Psychological studies have shown that when making a decision we tend to think we are more ethical than we really are (Tenbrunsel and Messick 2004). This combined with an over-confidence in one's analysis skills may lead to hasty judgment in relating evidence or giving more credibility to unreliable frail evidence. As we have indicated above, this overconfidence is added to by a tendency to give too much confidence to results coming out of a computer-decision support system designed to aid visual thinking. There are two ways to deal with this danger of high confidence in weak decisions. One is to introduce social sanctions on the analyst. A second method is to introduce provenance and the need to explicitly state the reason, i.e. empirical evidence. (Based 2010) The system cannot impose social sanctions so it must provide traceability for all decisions, i.e. decision provenance. The complexity of these systems is evident in that the attempt to resolve one form of bias may introduce another.

Thawing requirements and research projects In this research project several of the requirements were in flux and the various decisions on how to implement them could lead to very different ethical results. In this kind of project it is important not to underestimate the level of detail needed to make an ethical assessment; the level of detail needed to fill the 'gap' between technology development and soft human issues.

Steps Taken over the Course of the Project

The communication lines in the VALCRI ethics communications organised chart were too narrow. IEB would pass broad complex social concerns to management who would pass the concern on in summary form to developers who would try to interpret what was meant and then either try to implement their interpretation or might say 'it was not part of the project' in part because they did not want to spend a lot of time away from their "real" responsibilities. These difficulties were addressed by VALCRI in several ways. They made clear that mitigating the ethical issues was part of the "real work" and they widened the communications channels. IEB worked with SEPL and attended other working group meetings. VALCRI established additional sub-groups to co-ordinate work on linked themes. IEB was given access to all VALCRI documents and invited to prototype presentations and communications with user groups. The initial approach to addressing IEB concerns was one directional from IEB to developers, an approach which led to misunderstanding and wasted effort. The addition of a feedback mechanism was critical in moving forward. The positive support of management in asserting the importance of addressing these issues and providing vehicles to address them resulted in a more effective development process and better system, and negotiating through disagreements improves understanding and reduces the gap between the different interests (ethics advisors and developers). A full time experienced ethics specialist inside the project with the ability to physically visit the various development sites when ethical issues were found would be extremely useful for a similar project.

Conclusions

In this paper, we have attempted to set out the challenges faced in embedding 'ethics in design' for research and technical development projects. The path to achieving that has highlighted difficulties in communicating requirements from the ethics side to the development teams. Some of the methods for communication and managing the process of addressing the issues identified have been more successful than others. The 'translation' from ethics issues to implementing solutions was problematic, particularly at the beginning of the project, but the steps taken to overcome this in the formation of cross-cutting groups and discussions between the SEPL group and the different technical teams resulted in a significant improvement in the process and understanding.

Acknowledgement The VALCRI project has received funding from the European Union 7th Framework Programme (FP7/2007–2013) under grant agreement no FP7-IP- 608142, to Middlesex University and Partners.

References

Based, A. (2010). Information handling in security solution decisions. In S. Tarek (Ed.), *Innovations and advance in computer science and engineering*. Dordrecht, Springer.

Chen, C., & Koufas, M. (2015). The impact of decision support system features on user overconfidence and risky behavior. *European Journal of Informatics Systems, 24*(6), 607.

DOW. (2014). Description of Work, VALCRI project. Internal document (contact B.L.W.Wong).

Haider, J., Pohl, M., Hillemann, E.-C., Nussbaumer, A., Attfield, S., Passmore, P., & Wong, B. L. W. (2015). Exploring the challenges of implementing guidelines for the design of visual analytics systems. *Proceedings of the Human Factors and Ergonomics Society 59th Annual Meeting, 59*(1), 259–263, Sage.

IEB. (2017). Independent ethics board second report on VALCRI project. The Midterm Report to European Commission January 2017. Second Mid-Term Project Review (2017) (MTR 2) D4.6 "D4.6UIDesign for Provenance and Uncertainty Final".

Islam, J., Anslow, C., Xu, K., & Wong, B. L. W. (2017). Analytical provenance for criminal intelligence analysis. VALCRI White Paper Series. Available from: http://valcri.org/our-content/uploads/2017/02/VALCRI-WP-2017-009-Provenance3.pdf. Accessed 30 Nov 2017.

Millitello, L. (2017). Applying NDM to change behavior and persuade" 13th international conference on naturalistic decision making 2017, Bath, UK.

Schlehahn, E., Duquenoy, P., Paudyal, P., George, C., Coudert, F., Delvaux, A., & Marquenie, T. (2017). The operationalisation of transparency in VALCRI. VALCRI white Paper Series, 2017. Available from: http://valcri.org/our-content/uploads/2017/02/VALCRI-WP-2017-005-Transparency.pdf. Accessed 30 Nov 2017.

Shepherd, I. (2015). Single Vision Statement of Goals. 2 June 2015 Krakow Consortium meeting.

Tenbrunsel, A., & Messick, D. (2004). Ethical fading: The role of self-deception in unethical behavior. *Social Justice Research June, 2004,* 223–236.

Open Access This chapter is licensed under the terms of the Creative Commons Attribution 4.0 International License (http://creativecommons.org/licenses/by/4.0/), which permits use, sharing, adaptation, distribution and reproduction in any medium or format, as long as you give appropriate credit to the original author(s) and the source, provide a link to the Creative Commons license and indicate if changes were made.

The images or other third party material in this chapter are included in the chapter's Creative Commons license, unless indicated otherwise in a credit line to the material. If material is not included in the chapter's Creative Commons license and your intended use is not permitted by statutory regulation or exceeds the permitted use, you will need to obtain permission directly from the copyright holder.

Chapter 5
Evaluating the Ability and Desire of Police and Crime Commissioners (PCCs) to Deliver Community-Oriented Policing in Practice

John L. M. McDaniel

The Police and Crime Commissioner (PCC) model of police governance and accountability was established in England and Wales in 2012 in an effort to realise an ethos of community-oriented policing. The new PCC model promised to replace the 'invisible and unaccountable Police Authorities and make the police accountable to a directly-elected individual who will set policing priorities for local communities' (HAC 2016, p.3). The Police Authorities, in use since 1964, were part-time committees of councillors and magistrates who were expected to hold chief constables to account but were widely considered to be amateurish, unorganised, 'unaccountable, uncontactable and frankly unknown' (ibid, p.17–18). Under the watch of Police Authorities, police forces had reportedly lost sight of the community-oriented function of public policing and had become 'disconnected from the communities they serve', 'bogged down by bureaucracy' and answerable 'to distant politicians' (HAC 2010, p.3). Although they regularly adopted the rhetoric of 'community-oriented policing', chief constables and their subordinate officers were criticised for continuing to under-appreciate the individual and collective senses of insecurity within the community by attaching too much weight to their own policing expertise (ibid).

The PCC model, in contrast, promised a return to community-oriented policing, which holds that civilians should be able to ask a police force to amend the conduct of its police officers, the deployment of its resources and its strategic and tactical policies in order to address community needs, wants, concerns and complaints (Manning 1978). Communities should be able to regulate the exercise of police discretion by encouraging police officers to narrow their exercise of discretion in areas of growing community concern or by applying a wider degree of discretion in

J. L. M. McDaniel (✉)
School of Social, Historical and Political Studies, Mary Seacole Building,
University of Wolverhampton, Wolverhampton, UK
e-mail: J.McDaniel@wlv.ac.uk

© The Author(s) 2018
G. Leventakis, M. R. Haberfeld (eds.), *Societal Implications of Community-Oriented Policing and Technology*, SpringerBriefs in Criminology,
https://doi.org/10.1007/978-3-319-89297-9_5

areas where hard policing tactics are perceived to be unfair or counterproductive (McDaniel 2017). Community-oriented policing requires police officers to be tolerant and sensitive to differing views and cultural, political and economic values espoused by multiple cultures (Loader and Mulcahy 2003). Every individual within a neighbourhood should be treated as a valued and distinctive service user, each with their own distinctive crime problems and resident concerns (Brogden and Nijar 2005). A community-oriented ethos should enable the police organisation to realise the ideal of 'policing by consent' and the traditional Peelian principle that the 'police are the public and the public are the police' in a pragmatic way. The police organisation should ultimately be able to point to local community consultation to explain, substantiate and validate their strategies, tactics and conduct (Manning 1978; Bayley and Shearing 1996; Walsh 1998; Jackson et al. 2012).

The appointment of a directly-elected individual to hold each police force to account was considered necessary to put police oversight back into the hands of the public, to counteract rising crime rates, and to reverse the tendency of some police forces to treat low-level offending with scant regard (Caless and Owens 2016). The ethos of community-oriented policing was so central to the new PCC model that it was embedded within the Police Reform and Social Responsibility Act 2011, which established the PCC model. More particularly, the Act held that the PCC, when carrying out any statutory functions, 'must have regard to the views of people in the body's area about policing in that area' (2011, s.17.1). Moreover, section 14 (amending s.96 of the Police Act 1996) states in no uncertain terms that '… arrangements shall be made for each police area for obtaining the views of people in that area about matters concerning the policing of the area, and their co-operation with the police in preventing crime in that area and for obtaining the views of victims of crime in that area about matters concerning the policing of the area'. A document referred to as a 'police and crime plan' was placed at the centre of this process. The Act held that 'the police and crime commissioner for a police area must issue a police and crime plan within the financial year in which each ordinary election is held' and that the plan must be issued 'as soon as practicable after the commissioner takes office' (2011, s.5.1 – s.5.4). The plan must set out: the commissioner's 'police and crime objectives' for crime and disorder reduction in that area, and the means by which the chief officer's performance will be measured, amongst other aspects (2011, s.7). It required the PCC to make arrangements to obtain 'the views of the people in that police area, and the views of the victims of crime in that area, on that plan' (ibid). The PCC, in turn, was to hold the chief constable 'to account for the exercise of the duty … to have regard to [the] police and crime plan' (2011, s.1). The police and crime plan was so central to the new model that one PCC stated that the only circumstances in which he would have considered using his powers of dismissal was if the chief constable had 'strayed from the police and crime plan' which would mean 'the force is not doing the job we are expecting it to do' (HAC 2016, p.13). Another PCC added that if his chief constable was asked to define his job in one sentence, he would say that 'I deliver the police and crime plan' (ibid, p.7).

An evaluation of the police and crime plans published by the Greater Manchester, the West Midlands and the London Metropolitan PCCs between 2013 and 2016 indicates that PCCs are embracing the ethos of community-oriented policing on face value. The police and crime plan for Greater Manchester for 2016/17, for example, states that the PCC will 'seek and reflect the views of the public and particularly victims of crime in setting policing priorities and holding the chief constable to account for the performance of the force' (2016, p. 21). The PCC also promises to investigate whether 'local policing and other public services operate in a way that is relevant to local communities, with an understanding of their needs and concerns' and whether the force has 'done its utmost to provide good customer care and levels of service' amongst other issues (ibid, p. 30–33). The plans for the West Midlands and Greater London use similar language throughout. The plan for the West Midlands (2015a, p.8), for instance, promises that communities will be put 'first', while the London Mayor's Office for Policing and Crime (MOPAC) promises to greatly 'enhance' neighbourhood policing (2013, p. 23).

Under ambitious headings such as 'increasing public confidence', 'reducing crime rates', 'creating more prosperous communities' and 'creating a new era in policing', one might expect that more practical, community-focused issues would be captured, explained and addressed within the police and crime plans. However, and quite remarkably, the police and crime plans do not get much more specific than this. Although PCCs typically arrange daily meetings or calls with their chief constables and receive summaries of crime occurrences and case progression, the plans contain no real mention of specific crimes which are inflicting particular neighbourhoods. Objectives such as: 'we will reduce burglary by focusing on the areas suffering from this crime ... [and] we will ensure that our communities are satisfied with the service they receive' lack specific details to guide police officers or members of the public (WMPCC 2013, p. 2–7). The plans are almost entirely devoid of specific workable information. The deliverables and objectives are not even close to being clear enough so that they can be broken down into tasks which are achievable and subsequently delegated to units who are capable of achieving them. More broadly, the police and crime plans do not contain crime reports, crime maps or threat assessments of local crime, terrorism, organised crime or cyber-crime. The benchmarks for public confidence, satisfaction, reporting, recording, complaint and inter-agency collaboration around victims and mental health are also largely generic. Not only are the PCCs' intentions vague but almost no attempt is made to translate aspirations into actions, methods or means (McDaniel 2018). The West Midlands police and crime plan, for instance, claims that the neighbourhood policing team emphasise 'consistency', 'continuity', 'engagement', 'communication', 'visibility' and 'community-led initiatives', 'neighbourhood watch' and 'developing specialist staff' but without the accompaniment of specific details these statements are little more than value-free rhetorical clichés. The West Midlands Police, for example, was found by the Independent Police Complaints Commission (IPCC 2014) to be mishandling 8 out of 10 cases relating to allegations of racial discrimination but no attempt was made to address this through a revised version of the police and crime plan. Bland statements such as 'we will ... continue our review of Force management and leadership' do not indicate whether and to what extent specific problems are being rectified (WMPCC 2015a, p.24).

Most importantly, there is limited evidence within the police and crime plans to suggest that the 'deliverables' are actually based upon community needs and wants. The plans make no clear attempt to pinpoint the concerns of particular neighbourhoods or reconcile a cross-section of views. When challenged by the Home Affairs Committee (2016), various PCCs admitted that they simply do not have the resources to communicate directly and effectively with the public. The police and crime plan for London (2013, p. 18–19), for example, stated that it was premised by and large on a town hall meeting in each of the 32 city boroughs which involved no more than 3000 people as well as an online survey, focus groups, forums and 'hundreds of written responses and … scores of community groups'. Moreover, MOPAC (2015) reported that it had received only 2470 enquiries from members of the public between April 2014 and April 2015. With a population of over eight million people, the involvement of only a few thousand people does not appear to amount to a representative sample or significant engagement in community consultation. Similarly, it was not unusual for monthly meetings of the West Midlands PCC's ad hoc Strategic Policing and Crime Board (2016) to report that 'there were no questions from the public or petitions received'.

Caless and Owens (2016), who conducted interviews with 23 (of 41) PCCs with a view to shedding some light on the attitudes of PCCs towards issues of police governance, community engagement, collaborative working and social media, were particularly critical of the attempts of PCCs at grassroots consultation. They found that PCCs who relentlessly engage in public encounters, whether face to face or through social media, do so 'merely to have more people recognise them and understand what they do, if they are lucky' (2016, p.148). They argued that the impact of social media work is particularly questionable since none of the PCCs they interviewed had considered 'surveying the impact of their social messaging … and whether or not the PCCs social messaging is reaching large numbers of young people' (ibid, p.137). They found that, in reality, serious commentary about society, the fear of crime and personal unease hardly figured in social media largely because the purpose of social messaging sites was about 'having fun and unwinding' (ibid, p.147). They concluded that the PCCs 'conviction that this is worth it sometimes borders on the desperate…' (ibid, p.148). Similarly, Lister and Rowe (2015) found that '…there are recurring questions over how the results of such consultations are interpreted and thereafter translated into practice'.

In terms of performance benchmarking, section 12 of the Police Reform and Social Responsibility Act 2011 requires the PCC to 'produce a report (an "annual report") on the exercise of the body's functions, and the progress which has been made in the financial year in meeting the police and crime objectives in the body's police and crime plan'. The data should reflect a true picture of the needs of the constituent communities and enable the persons who live in the area to assess the performance of the police organisation. Unfortunately, the annual reports are similarly vacuous. The West Midlands PCC (2015b) reported, for instance, that public place violence with injury had increased by almost 11 per cent (1048 offences) compared to 2013–2014, yet no explanation was provided for this increase and no immediate form of remedial action was identifiable. Similarly, no attempt was made to explain why there had been a 'step change up' for some crime occurrences, whether 'stable' crime occurrences were acceptable and what the PCC was planning to do about such developments (WMPCC 2015b). In addition, public confidence was reported to be at 82% and satisfaction with service was at 82.8% in 2015 but no attempt was made to explain why almost 20% of the population did not have full confidence in the police (ibid). In Greater Manchester, the 'Report of the Chief Constable to the Commissioner for Greater Manchester' (2013) told quite a different story to the PCC's annual report of the same year. The PCC did not attempt to explain the reasons behind or convey the chief constable's explanation for a 'significant' 19% increase in crimes of theft from the person; a 'significant' increase of 18% in sexual offences; a 'significant' increase of 10% in incidents of anti-social behaviour or the fact that only 23% of victim-based crimes had been solved in the previous 12 months (ibid, p.4–9). The chief constable, however, presented these figures and tried to explain the reasons behind them in his report, whereas the PCC's (2013) annual report did not mention many of the issues. In comparison to the chief constable's report, the PCC's publication was considerably uninformative and arguably misleading.

The lack of proactive public engagement on the part of PCCs is lamentable considering the fact that voluminous academic research indicates that it is not unusual for some communities to be systemically averse to community-police dialogue out of hostility and distrust caused by prolonged periods of over-policing, abusive practices, perceived prejudices and generational neglect (Scarman 1981). Unfortunately, the Police Reform and Social Responsibility Act 2011 is silent on the forms, frequency and methods of community-engagement which PCCs should employ. Whether and to what extent a PCC engages in wide reaching consultation or communication remains largely a discretionary decision, unique to each individual PCC. In the absence of a more structured apparatus, it would appear that section 14, which requires the PCC to obtain 'the views of people in that area about matters concerning the policing of the area ... and the views of victims of crime in that area', is only being paid lip-service. Lister and Rowe (2015) found that some PCCs will engage in a measure of community consultation 'rather hurriedly' and only when they are required to do so 'shortly after coming into office (i.e. once every four years)'. Similarly, the Stevens Commission (2013, p.81) found that 'there is little evidence to indicate ... that PCCs are engaging successfully with diverse communities across their constituencies'.

Instead of realising the ethos of community-oriented policing in practice, it would appear that various PCCs are pursuing the interests of 'public relations' over and above 'community relations'. 'Public relations', in this context, involves the promotion of a superficial public image of policing whereas 'community relations' involves learning about the needs of minority groups and adapting police procedures to provide a reassuring police service for all (Banton 1973; Mawby 2002). The interviews carried out by Caless and Owens (2016) indicate that PCCs are cognisant of the power of superficial 'image work'. One PCC told them that '...thinly attended meetings in cold village community centres don't do it for me. I'd rather be filmed talking to someone in a shopping centre or in a town square. Better visually and better in terms of media attention' (ibid, p. 145). Another interviewee said that '... what the audience doesn't see is that his [the PCC's] message is the same each time (I could certainly repeat it word-for-word): hold cops to account, reduce crime, increase and support neighbourhood teams, reassurance, cut anti-social behaviour, cope with budget cuts, prevent crime, care for the environment and the rest...' (ibid, p. 152). One chief officer eloquently surmised that the PCC 'seems to find it hard to step outside his restatement of the clichés that got him returned to office ... what he hasn't got across to the public is what he has actually achieved in any of his platforms' (ibid, p. 203).

As Mawby (2002) conveys, police forces should be image conscious and engage in image management but such 'image work' must be based on the ethical and effective conduct of its police officers during interactions and engagements with the public rather than a fictitious presentation of policing which is designed for public consumption. The presentation of a fictitious account of police performance and community attitudes in place of police-community partnership inevitably leads to perverse forms of policing and police governance. Statements such as 'I represent the voice of the public', 'I am the voice of the people' and 'I represent all the people' can lead to the self-promotion of PCCs' personal virtue ethics and political ideals, absent of wider community consultation and representation. A degree of self-grandiosity amongst PCCs was identified by Lister and Rowe (2015) who examined the election statements of all 41 successful candidates and found that only 58.5% of the statements mentioned 'consultation with the public', which is one of their primary statutory responsibilities. They concluded that 'there was no evidence in the election statements of [some] incoming PCCs that such a discussion was even anticipated' (ibid).

The indicative result is that there does not appear to be sufficient community input, leading to commensurate community-oriented outputs. The apparatus appears to be wholly inadequate for the purposes of community consultation. Communities are arguably having a negligible effect on the shape and form of police policies and priorities as a result. Nor are PCCs presenting the public with fulsome and regular assessments of outcomes and evidence of their impact on community crime problems. The participatory and deliberative conception of policing, which was initially hoped for, appears to have been replaced by the tendency of PCCs to employ language and rhetoric within their plans which presents a politically desirable image of discursive policing but without the substance. Vague mission statements like 'we serve our community' and 'we listen to our citizens', which were traditionally employed by chief officers to the frustrations of civilians, have simply become the preserve of another remote political vehicle. The police and crime plans would appear to be little more than a reflection of the PCCs' own social philosophies rather than clear community-led initiatives which can guide and shape the form and style of police activities and civilian interactions. Instead of establishing clear means which can be measured and assessed, which the 2011 Act demands, PCCs have done little other than creatively wrap up these basic requirements within a number of ambiguous themes and rhetorical clichés. The frequent absence of specific, tangible actions and considerations appears to reflect a lack of seriousness of PCCs towards their statutory responsibilities and community-oriented policing more broadly. It is submitted that the wide disparities between the police and crime plans and police developments on the ground; the lack of improvement over time and the absence of community consultation serves to fundamentally discredit the PCCs' claims to community-oriented policing in reality.

Conclusion

Rather than heralding a new era of explanatory accountability, it appears that the 'communicative gap' which exists between the police and the communities they serve is widening (Loader and Mulcahy 2003). The dominance of the PCC's personality appears to recreate many of the problems associated with the professional police attitude of the 1970s. PCCs, like the chief officers and police authorities before them, now appear to believe that they know what is best for the community without actually asking. The ethos of community-oriented policing, which was developed in the 1970s to explicitly counteract this professional police mind-set (Manning 1978), has spawned the very form of insular police governance that it was designed to counteract. The experiment has been reduced, by some PCCs, to little more than a superficial public relations exercise which promotes an assumed degree of civic participation but without the substance. Rather than building strong police-community relationships through communication, transparency and accountability, PCCs appear to be relying primarily on the individual and positional power granted to them by statute to give policing the veneer of community-oriented policing rather than the reality of it.

References

Banton, M. (1973). *Police – Community relations*. Willan Publishing.
Bayley, D., & Shearing, C. (1996). The future of policing. *Law & Society Review, 30*(3), 585–606.
Brogden, M., & Nijar, P. (2005). *Community policing: National and international models and approaches*. Willan.
Caless, B., & Owens, J. (2016). *Police and crime commissioners: The transformation of police accountability*. Policy Press.
GMPCC. (2013). *Report on the police and crime plan*. Office of the Police and Crime Commissioner for Greater Manchester.
GMPCC. (2016). *Police and crime plan 2016–2017*. Office of the Police and Crime Commissioner for Greater Manchester.
Greater Manchester Police. (2013). Report to the police and crime commissioner on the *Force Delivery Plan*. November 2013.
HAC. (2010). Policing: Police and crime commissioners, House of Commons Home Affairs Committee Second Report of Session 2010–11, HC511.

HAC. (2016). Police and crime commissioners: Here to stay. House of Commons Home Affairs Committee Seventh Report of Session 2015–16, HC844.

IPCC. (2014). Police handling of allegations of discrimination. Independent Police Complaints Commission.

Jackson, J., et al. (2012). Why do people comply with the law. *British Journal of Criminology, 52*, 1051–1071.

Lister, S., & Rowe, M. (2015). Electing police and crime commissioners in England and Wales: Prospecting for the democratisation of policing. *Policing and Society, 25*, 4.

Loader, I., & Mulcahy, A. (2003). *Policing and the condition of England: Memory, politics and culture*. Oxford: Oxford University Press.

Manning, P. K. (1978). The police mandate: Strategies and appearances. In P. K. Manning & J. Van Maanen (Eds.), *Poliscing: A view from the streets*. New York: Random House.

Mawby, R. (2002). *Policing images: Policing, communication and legitimacy*. Willan Publishing.

McDaniel, J. L. M. (2017). Rethinking the law and politics of democratic police accountability. *The Police Journal: Theory, Practice and Principles*. https://doi.org/10.1177/0032258X16685107.

McDaniel, J. L. M. (2018). Reconciling mental health, public policing and police accountability. The Police Journal: Theory, Practice and Principles. https://doi.org/10.1177/00322 58X18766372.

MOPAC. (2013). *Police and crime plan 2013–2016*. London: The Mayor's Office for Policing and Crime.

MOPAC. (2015). *Annual report 2014/15*. London: The Mayor's Office for Policing and Crime.

Scarman, L. (1981). *The Scarman report: The Brixton disorders*. London: HMSO.

Stevens Commission. (2013). Policing for a Better Britain. Report of the Independent Police Commission. The Lord Stevens of Kirkwhelpington QPM.

Walsh, D. P. J. (1998). The Irish Police: A legal and constitutional perspective. Roundhall Sweet and Maxwell.

West Midlands Strategic Policing and Crime Board. (2016). *Performance against the 2015–16 milestones and deliverables in the Police and Crime Plan*. Birmingham City Council House, Birmingham. 7 June 2016.

WMPCC. (2013). Local policing plan Birmingham. Office of the Police and Crime Commissioner for the West Midlands Police.

WMPCC. (2015a). The west midlands police and crime plan: Pride in our police 2015/16. Office of the Police and Crime Commissioner for the West Midlands Police.

WMPCC. (2015b). Annual Report 2014–15. Office of the Police and Crime Commissioner for the West Midlands Police.

Open Access This chapter is licensed under the terms of the Creative Commons Attribution 4.0 International License (http://creativecommons.org/licenses/by/4.0/), which permits use, sharing, adaptation, distribution and reproduction in any medium or format, as long as you give appropriate credit to the original author(s) and the source, provide a link to the Creative Commons license and indicate if changes were made.

The images or other third party material in this chapter are included in the chapter's Creative Commons license, unless indicated otherwise in a credit line to the material. If material is not included in the chapter's Creative Commons license and your intended use is not permitted by statutory regulation or exceeds the permitted use, you will need to obtain permission directly from the copyright holder.

Chapter 6
Social Media and Community Policing Implementation in South Eastern Europe: A Question of Trust

Janina Czapska and Katarzyna Struzińska

I. Community policing (COP) is based on close and frequent police–community interactions aimed at solving local security problems. In recent years, a use of social media (SM) within this model of police work increasingly gains in importance (Denef et al. 2012: 22–24). Nevertheless, in post-communist societies, where COP is still relatively new, the use of SM by the police might face challenges related to insufficient public confidence in the law enforcement, and stereotypical negative image of the police officers, who are perceived as more control- than community-oriented.

In this context, SM seem to be a tool that might support the process of improving the police image what, consequently, can lead to an increase of citizens' trust. Owing to the fact that SM enable users to play an active role in the public discourse, they might be an effective measure to bridge gaps in relations between the police and citizens. SM can foster the development of participatory culture by simplifying police–community contact as well as by enabling an effective two-way communication.

In this paper, we analyse chosen quantitative research on police legitimacy, as well as present findings of our field studies in Bosnia and Herzegovina (BiH) which are a part of the EU funded international research project *Community-Based Policing and Post-Conflict Police Reform* (ICT4COP; 2015–2020). The empirical part of the paper is based on the chosen qualitative data gathered during research in BiH in 2016.

Author contributed equally to this paper. Janina Czapska and Katarzyna Struzińska

J. Czapska · K. Struzińska (✉)
Department of Sociology of Law, Faculty of Law, Jagiellonian University, Kraków, Poland
e-mail: katarzyna.struzinska@uj.edu.pl

© The Author(s) 2018
G. Leventakis, M. R. Haberfeld (eds.), *Societal Implications of Community-Oriented Policing and Technology*, SpringerBriefs in Criminology,
https://doi.org/10.1007/978-3-319-89297-9_6

II. Police legitimacy is the declared, or at least presumed, aim of COP implementation that gains particular importance while implementing this strategy in post-communist countries. Reaching a high level of police legitimacy is connected to an array of positive outcomes, among which we can list enhancing readiness to cooperate with the police and readiness to obey the law. Legitimacy is a permanently under-defined notion. The most general definition frames it as 'the right to rule and the recognition by the ruled of that right' (e.g. Hough et al. 2013: 4). In this initial differentiation is hidden the basic distinction between normative (objective) legitimacy and empirical (subjective) legitimacy. In the normative understanding, legitimacy indicates whether the police meet certain desirable standards (mainly in the framings of lawyers and political philosophers). Police legitimacy in the subjective (empirical) understanding consists in the conviction of the ruled that the ruling has the right to express orders that have to be obeyed.

A challenge for researchers and social politicians is to define what the relation between legitimacy in the normative understanding and in the empirical one can be (is/should be). It is of particular importance in societies undergoing transformation, as at that moment, they often experience anomy and abrupt ideological or legal changes. The history of many such countries demonstrates how dynamically police legitimacy may vary due to political changes.

III. Owing to the growing interest in these issues, today we could announce the coming of an era of 'legitimacy of the police' as research problem undertaken with unprecedented frequency. The differences between particular studies concern the understandings of legitimacy, the relation between legitimacy and trust to the police, the factors that affect legitimacy. The relations between these factors are usually presupposed by researchers in initial models (hypotheses), and the real connections are established on the basis of empirical data.

The diagnosed connections should be the basis for political and legal proposals as to what should be done to reinforce police legitimacy in particular societies. Obviously, it cannot be expected that by using right, context-rooted arguments, according to the assumptions of evidence-based policing, one single right solution can be chosen. Unfortunately, it is not the only problem, as the analysis of studies accessible in mid-2017 leads to the conclusion that the understandings of each of the studied factors become increasingly unclear, and the possibility of comparing or formulating hypotheses on the basis of existing studies is decreasing.

The analysis of the ways in which studies frame the relations between such variables as: trust to the police, legitimacy, legality of action, procedural justice, distributive justice, efficiency of the police, sharing common values with the police, readiness to cooperate with the police, legal cynicism, behaviours compliant with the law, sense of obligation to obey orders, leads to the conclusion that questionnaires often ask the same questions and only in the statistical analysis of the results the answers are linked to one another and labelled differently.

It seems that researchers agree as to the 'account of the dynamic and interactive nature of legitimacy' (Bottoms and Tankebe 2012); the dialogue continues between the police and the society. It is very challenging to attempt to answer the question whether, while trying to establish what legitimacy is, what factors affect it and what outcomes it may have, it is possible to distinguish specific features of post-conflict countries in a methodologically correct way with the current state of knowledge. The most important ways of arriving at the answers as to what legitimacy of the police is can be characterized in the following way on the basis of exemplary research carried out in the past few years:

(a) The concept of police legitimacy constructed for the fifth round (R5) of the research conducted in EU member states for the European Social Survey (ESS) is based on the assumption that perceived legitimacy could be understood as a multi-dimensional concept involving consent (the obligation to obey the police), moral alignment (sharing common values by the citizens and the police) and lawfulness (legality of the police actions). 'Trust' is not an element of 'legitimacy' but trust to select aspects of the police/the police officers' actions can influence the level of legitimacy. The research distinguished trust to: procedural justice, distributive justice, and the police efficiency.

Comparing the answers to particular questions in these studies does not allow us to determine a clear profile of the so-called post-communist countries but in particular questions differences between this category of countries and other countries can be noticed. In other cases, the citizens of the so-called post-communist countries give answers identical to those of the citizens of e.g. Southern European ones. However, the method of analysis, consisting in applying multiple factors of certain constructs should be used with great caution, as 'a lack of evidence potentially compromises any substantive cross-national comparisons' (Jackson et al. 2013: 188). In the analysed studies, it turned out that the strongest influence on each component of legitimacy was exercised by procedural justice.

(b) Research on police legitimacy in Central and Eastern Europe (CEE) with the participation of Bosnia and Herzegovina and Serbia have been conducted so far usually among students of higher school; the first research was carried out in 2013 among law students coming from eight countries of CEE (Meško et al. 2016; Lukić et al. 2016). Police legitimacy was deemed there to be a two-element concept (felt obligation and trust in the police) and other variables connected to this issue were taken into consideration as well, in particular: procedural justice, the police efficiency, distributive justice, the probability of sanction, moral credibility, legal cynicism, and the following were assumed as potential outcomes: cooperation with the police, readiness to obey the law.

A comparison of the countries indicates statistically significant differences among all countries for: police legitimacy, the police efficiency, willingness to cooperate with the police, procedural justice and moral credibility (Lukić et al. 2016: 426). The authors of the research explained that legitimacy and trust in the police are related to the state of democracy in the studied countries (Meško et al. 2016: 79–80), which was analysed more in-depth on the example of differences between Slovenia and Serbia which had reformed their police differently. However, it was observed that: 'It is surprising that both student groups have a similar opinion about the police in their countries.' (Lukić et al. 2016: 433). An explanation as to what role is played in forming opinions by historical, systemic and cultural differences between particular societies can be brought by further studies. Similarly to the ESS, almost in all countries of CEE, the strongest influence on subjective police legitimacy and its particular components was exercised by procedural justice. Some later research with the use of the same method has also been carried out among students from Sarajevo (Muratbegović et al. 2014).

(c) In the study of Serbian students conducted in 2014 (Zekavica and Kesetovic 2015), the initial model comprised ten aspects of legitimacy which were then operationalized usually with questions used in previously conducted studies, but the variables created on their basis were labelled in different ways. The most important aspects of the way in which students perceive police legitimacy are: their perception of the distribution of the police services, the nature and the quality of those services, the perception of the police, the confidence in the police work, and, finally, the perception of the legality of the police work; obedience (felt obligation) was not included in this research category (Zekavica and Kesetovic 2015: 39).

IV. In conclusion, the analysis of the research and of the used models of police legitimacy does not provide a satisfying answer to the questions what legitimacy is, what it depends on, what it influences in particular societies, and what is its relation to trust to the police. However, it allows us to notice the variety of approaches and formulate questions for further research. Among them, the most important are: the role and understanding of trust to the police; possible differentiation between general trust to the police and trust to particular aspects of their work; roles played in forming police legitimacy by the opinions on the police effectiveness and its fulfillment of the conditions of procedural or distributive justice. In countries in transformation, it is important to consider the significance of 'legal cynicism', to determine how it influences the process of forming attitudes towards the police and, in particular, on readiness to cooperate with them. In search for specific features, it is also worth verifying the thesis that the efficiency of social institutions has a significant impact on the perception of legitimacy in these countries (Lukić et al. 2016: 422). In the case of societies in transformation, the problem lies in the re-definition of the basic role of the police. We believe that the most significant change which has been taking place was the one from a 'force' to a 'service' orientation. Consolidating the conviction that the police's role is that of a service-provider, and it is not an 'authority,' as militia had been treated previously, in the social consciousness is emblematic in the process of the police's development in countries that undergo transformation.

It is of utmost importance to determine what role is played by the type and quality of contacts with the police in forming their legitimacy. It seems that hitherto only contacts of a direct character of victims or witnesses have been studied, little attention has been paid in the process of studying police legitimacy in the context of communication via Internet, and via SM in specific. Particular attention needs to be paid to adolescents, for whom the virtual reality is usually a 'natural' environment. At the same time, some specific characteristics of adolescents need to be taken into consideration, in particular, an 'anti-authority syndrome' (Lukić et al. 2016: 422).

The state of knowledge on police legitimacy and building trust to them via SM has an array of weaknesses – we know too little about it, as the studies conducted so far in South Eastern Europe concerned mostly students. Also, they were of quantitative character; it seems then that research on legitimacy is dominated by statistics. We still know very little about what both sides of the interaction, that is the police and the citizens, think about using the media in mutual relations. Are SM mainly supposed to help the society control the police, form the police's image, or just serve as a channel of information? These still unclear questions will be analysed on the basis of our qualitative studies in Bosnia and Herzegovina.

V. Within the ICT4COP project, 59 in-depth interviews with experts from state, entity and community level institutions have so far taken place in BiH. The key goal of this article is to present these research results which are related to information and communication technology (ICT), in particular, to the ways in which social media have been so far and might be in the future used by the police. For the purpose of this article, we decided to limit a scope of our empirical analysis and concentrate it on one of two main entities with an extensive autonomy of which BiH consists, namely, on Federation of Bosnia and Herzegovina (FBiH).

Results presented in this paper come from 25 in-depth interviews conducted in FBiH. 11 of them were conducted with respondents representing various state, entity and cantonal level institutions, both public and nongovernmental, in Sarajevo. At the local level, two venues of a different character were studied in the same canton. In the first one, a rural municipality, 4 interviews took place. In the other, an urban municipality, 10 interviews with 11 respondents were conducted.

VI. All interviews in FBiH were conducted in line with the same, beforehand prepared guidelines. Regardless the level at which research was conducted, during each interview some questions about ICT were asked (e.g. questions about typical ways of communication between the police and citizens; specific ICT tools used by the police to communicate with citizens; opinions on the ICT influence on police–community relations, possible ICT solutions which should be used by the police in the future). All respondents were asked at least two questions about ICT; most frequently they answered questions about ways of police–citizen communication and ICT tools used by the police. Taking into account that ICT tools are only one of many possible ways of communication, we decided to start the part of interview dedicated to ICT with checking what the most popular forms of police–community interactions are. This general question was aimed at checking if respondents will describe only traditional ways of police–citizens communication, or they will spontaneously start to talk about modern communication solutions. Answers given by most of the interviewees, regardless the type of institution they represented, were consistent and indicated that police–community communication still takes mainly traditional forms, and happens mostly in the context of an offence being perpetrated.

Majority of respondents named phone calls as the main mean of exchanging information between the community and the police – it was noticed that citizens are rather reluctant to contact the police, and in most cases, they do this only when they have to report a crime. In such a context telephone was claimed to be the fastest way to contact the police. According to the majority of respondents, the other widespread form of police-community communication is face to face communication, which can be initiated not only by the citizens but also by police officers. Almost a half of respondents noticed as well that it might be possible to contact the police via police's web pages and to get some information from them. Nevertheless, it has to be noticed that the police in these parts of FBiH where our research was conducted do not have own official web pages and the Internet sources to which the interviewees referred were in fact portals of ministries of interiors – institutions to which police forces are subordinated. SM were mentioned only once in the context of monitoring them by the police to glean some useful information.

After giving the broader context of the most popular ways in which the police and community exchange information, interviewees were asked about ICT tools that are used by the police to communicate with citizens and to inform them. Respondents who already named some ICT solutions were asked if they know any other tools used by the police. Interviewees most often pointed out the Krimolovci [crime catchers] hotline which enables citizens in the whole country to call the police anonymously and for free to provide them with relevant information. Moreover, relatively frequently web pages of the police, in fact again portals of ministries of interior, and e-mails were named among answers. None of the respondents mentioned spontaneously that the police use SM to communicate with citizens.

All respondents who were asked in specific about SM claimed that they have not been so far used by the police as a mean of communication or that they do not have any knowledge about that. The most frequent answers show that ICT tools used in police–citizens interactions are based on one-sided mechanism of providing the other side with some (potentially) important pieces of information. It seems that for the police in FBiH there is a still some room for improvements when it comes to a full and active use of the interactive communication possibilities which occurred with the development of modern ICT, especially, of SM.

VII. The use of social media was most thoroughly commented in three cases: (1) by respondents from the police agencies when they talked about obstacles related to this mean of communication; by all respondents, regardless institutions they represented, (2) when they elaborated on the ways Bosnian citizens use SM to communicate with each other about their insecurities, and (3) when they presented opinions about potential impact which SM could have on police–community relations in FBiH.

Firstly, it was noticeable that some police representatives tended to perceive SM usage as a source of new problems for their agency. On the one hand, creating a chance for citizens to communicate with the police in a less formal way via SM was associated with a risk of getting many pieces of facetious or irrelevant information, which would cause an additional and often fruitless work for police officers. On the other hand, some of these respondents seemed reluctant to accept SM because they put the police 'more under observation, and under control' of citizens – any behaviour of a police officer can be easily recorded and publish e.g. on Facebook or YouTube. Nevertheless, for some local police officers, the potential use of SM in their daily work was rather abstract, due to the fact that at their police stations access to the Internet is limited or lacking.

Secondly, the majority of respondents emphasized that Bosnian citizens, in particular, young people, rather commonly use SM, especially Facebook, to communicate with each other. One of the respondents as an important aspect of this communication named an ability to create a 'critical mass' of people who '(…) meet up at the social networks in order to react'. Owing to the fact that SM are interactive and easily connect people who are interested in similar issues, they are often used by citizens to create networks which advocate solution of different security-related local problems.

Finally, when asked about the ICT tools which should be used to improve police–citizens relations, respondents, especially ones not related to the police, often pointed out that establishing official police social media profiles will have a positive impact on those relations. Interviewees often connected making communication via SM possible with the police becoming more open, transparent and easier to approach. Our research showed that two-way communication in SM is believed to be profitable for both citizens and the police. On the one hand, it gives citizens an easier and more direct way to access the police, not (or not only) in case of emergency, but primarily when they want to share their opinions, ask for advice or find some information. On the other hand, the police can become more visible thanks to SM which can serve them as a new source of knowledge about citizens' needs and opinions as well as a new channel of communication. Furthermore, some respondents noticed that the use of SM can positively influence the image of the police by giving citizens more insight into the police work, as well as by sharing with them some police success stories. In this context, SM seem to be a communication tool which brings the police and the community closer together, and as such, they can play a role in enhancing citizens' trust in the police.

Nevertheless, our research indicates also that despite the potential positive influence of social media on police–community relations, they are not a sufficient tool to increase the trust in the police. Some representatives of international organizations noticed that ICT tools will significantly improve the police–citizens communication only if they are 'built on trust'. Community members who distrust the police will not trust the ICT tools which are used by the police, and will not use them. Our research showed that police have to open up to citizens in the real world to make the best use of the opportunities which are offered by the virtual reality. Some of our respondents believe that to make SM a more effective communication platform, the process of trust building should 'start in the offline world'.

VIII. Expectations, challenges, and hopes related to the potential introduction of social media as a new mean of police–citizens communication in FBiH, which were revealed during our research, reflect the broader spectrum of the issues which are present in the literature on policing and SM. These media can serve the police as a new way to actively connect with the citizens. Due to the fact that they can not only be used to disseminate information but also to initiate both interaction and dialogue that might lead to real cooperation, they seem to be an innovative way to approach COP programmes. Our results are consistent with remarks made by Bain et al. (2014) on the beneficial role which SM can play in building and maintaining a positive image of the police. This role can be pivotal especially in post-communist societies which often need to deal with the insufficient level of police legitimacy. SM seem to be a useful tool which might be used by the police not only as a 'source of criminal information', but also for many other purposes, for instance: transmitting information, interacting and having a two-way communication with citizens or 'showing human side of policing' (cf. Denef et al. 2012: 12–26).

In the presented article we tried to show how various is the empirical image of the legitimacy itself, as well as the relation between police legitimacy and trust in the police. New research studies are necessary to fill the gaps in knowledge about key factors influencing the formation of police legitimacy, especially about police efficiency and procedural justice. Furthermore, the variety of different variables analysed in the research should be taken into account, while setting the aims and methods of police use of SM to communicate with citizens.

54   J. Czapska and K. Struzińska

Acknowledgement The *Community-Based Policing and Post-Conflict Police Reform (ICT4COP)* project presented in this paper received funding from the European Commission, under the call H2020-FCT-2014, Topic FCT-14-2014 Ethical/Societal Dimension TOPIC 2: Enhancing cooperation between law enforcement agencies and citizens – Community policing, under grant agreement number 653909.

References

Bain, A., Robinson, B. K., & Conser, J. (2014). Perceptions of policing: improving communication in local communities. *International Journal of Police Science & Management, 17*(4), 267–276.

Bottoms, A., & Tankebe, J. (2012). Beyond procedural justice: A dialogic approach to legitimacy in criminal justice. *Journal of Criminal Law & Criminology, 102*, 119–170.

Denef, S., Kaptein, N., Bayerl, P. S., & Ramirez, L. (2012). *Best practice in police social media adaptation.* COMPOSITE Project. https://administracionelectronica.gob.es/dam/jcr:e03b0d77-ed32-4f70-9071-cb6a523236ca/COMPOSITE-social-media-best-practice_1_.pdf.; http://www.composite-project.eu/index.php/1455/items/best-practice-in-police-social-media-adaptation-second-report-on-technology-adaption.html.

Hough, M., Jackson, J., & Bradford, B. (2013). Legitimacy, trust and compliance: An empirical test of procedural justice theory using the European Social Survey. In J. Tankebe & A. Liebling (Eds.), *Legitimacy and criminal justice: An international exploration* (pp. 326–352). Oxford: Oxford University Press.

Jackson, J., Kuha, J., Hough, M., Bradford, B., Hohl, K., & Gerber, M. M. (2013). *Trust and legitimacy across Europe: A FIDUCIA report on comparative public attitudes towards legal authority.*

Lukić, N., Bajović, V., Tičar, B., & Eman, K. (2016). Trust in police by Serbian and Slovenian law students: A comparative perspective. *Varstvoslovje, Journal of Criminal Justice and Security, 18*(4), 418–437.

Meško, G., Fields, C. B., Šifrer, J., & Eman, K. (2016). Understanding trust in police and legitimacy in Central Eastern Europe: The law student survey. In D. Nogala, K. Neidhardt, T. Görgen, J. Kersten, J.-M. Fiquet, & G. Meško (Eds.), *Policing civil societies in times of economic constraints: European police science and research bulletin (Special conference edition)* (pp. 73–80). Münster: European Police College (CEPOL).

Muratbegović, E., Vujović, S., & Fazlić, A. (2014). Procedural justice, police legitimacy and cooperation of Bosnian students with the police. *VARSTVOSLOVJE, Journal of Criminal Justice and Security, 16*(4), 387–411.

Zekavica, R., & Kesetovic, Z. (2015). The legitimacy of the police in Serbia. *Journal of Criminalistics and Law, 3*, 19–44.

Open Access This chapter is licensed under the terms of the Creative Commons Attribution 4.0 International License (http://creativecommons.org/licenses/by/4.0/), which permits use, sharing, adaptation, distribution and reproduction in any medium or format, as long as you give appropriate credit to the original author(s) and the source, provide a link to the Creative Commons license and indicate if changes were made.

The images or other third party material in this chapter are included in the chapter's Creative Commons license, unless indicated otherwise in a credit line to the material. If material is not included in the chapter's Creative Commons license and your intended use is not permitted by statutory regulation or exceeds the permitted use, you will need to obtain permission directly from the copyright holder.

Chapter 7
Use of Apps for Crime Reporting and the EU General Data Protection Regulation

Christina Charitou, Dimitrios G. Kogias, Spyros E. Polykalas, Charalampos Z. Patrikakis, and Ioana Cristina Cotoi

Introduction

With the number of Internet enabled devices (e.g., a smartphone, a tablet, a wearable or a laptop) highly increasing, so does their role in every person's daily life. Through the use of a call, an instant message, a post on social media or even real-time video communication, users can easily use their smartphone to report an event, ask for assistance or provide information about their status, allowing the provision of faster and more efficient safety services. To this end, community policing has come to be considered as a new and improved mode of policing by many countries in the past years.

In general, this new approach includes an increasingly active role of civilians in community policing which firstly includes to assist the police in creating improved relations with the communities they serve; and secondly, yet not unrelated, to make policing the responsibility of all members of a community which in turn should serve to decrease the level of crime in their society. In order to achieve this, the police service and communities need to have close working relationships with one another based on trust, transparency and a shared concern for safety, peace and stability. To facilitate the communication, the use of smart apps in Crime Reporting appears to be a fast and effective way of getting citizens engaged.

C. Charitou · D. G. Kogias · C. Z. Patrikakis (✉)
University of West Attica, Electronics Engineering Department, Egaleo, Greece
e-mail: charitou@puas.gr; dimikog@puas.gr; bpatr@puas.gr

S. E. Polykalas
TEI of Ionian Islands, Digital Media and Communication Department, Kefallonia, Greece

I. C. Cotoi
Engineering Ingegneria, Informatica, SPA, Lecce, Italy
e-mail: ioana.cotoi@eng.it

© The Author(s) 2018   55
G. Leventakis, M. R. Haberfeld (eds.), *Societal Implications of Community-Oriented Policing and Technology*, SpringerBriefs in Criminology,
https://doi.org/10.1007/978-3-319-89297-9_7

It goes without saying that police departments routinely collect information, while police reports include intimate details about victimization and other personal events. At the same time, the use of mobile applications in crime reporting will definitely lead to an increase of personal data collection and processing. These applications demand access to the user's personal data and information (e.g., location at the time of reporting via the embedded GPS sensor in the smartphone) for their efficient performance. By providing this access to his/her personal data, the user consents on the collection, storage and process of their data, hoping that this will be done in the frame to which he/she provided his/her consent.

But the sharing of certain consenting sensitive information is not, always, a bad thing. Especially when there are specific applications that aim at helping the user to increase the feeling of security in his/her everyday actions. Such applications are developed for smartphones, wearables and the web, in TRILLION (TRILLION Project 2017), that targets to enhance the role of community policing. The citizens will use the application both to report such events (e.g., vandalism actions in a concert, scenes right after an earthquake) in order to inform and update the LEAs about the conditions at the reported place, but also to communicate with registered users asking for help in crisis situation. To prevent any misuse, the personal data that are collected should follow the new regulation from the European Parliament, taking place from 2018, regarding the collection and process of personal data from the mobile applications.

To this end, Section 2 will try to describe the efforts that aim to enhance community policing (mainly in recent Security projects), while Section 3 will focus on the European GDPR and the way it affects the mobile applications Section 4 will describe the TRILLION use-case and how the applications that are developed for its performance can meet the new requirements, without affecting the TRILLION's system performance. In the last section, a conclusion about the noticeable points of this paper will be presented.

Related Work

The new data protection framework is based on the assumption that personal data processing is lawful only if this data is processed on the basis of the consent of the data subject concerned or some other legitimate basis, laid down by law: legal obligation, performance of a contract, vital interest of data subject or a third person, public interest or legitimate interests of the data controller or third persons. The GDPR preserves the purpose limitation principle as central element of the legal framework stating that data should be collected for specified, explicit and legitimate purposes and - principally - should not be processed for incompatible purposes. The Regulation confirmed the principles of accuracy and purpose-related duration of storage. Of utmost importance for a proportionate processing in the context of community policing is the data minimisation principle, which must be taken into consideration by the designing of the system.

Many solutions, that enhance the role of community (or neighborhood) policing, have been developed and applied lately with increasing interest and participation from the users. Next Door (NEXTDOOR n.d.) is an upcoming application that encourages the citizens of a neighbor to subscribe in an online system where they can register their neighbor and form a social network to circulate news. Xpose (Xpose n.d.) is another recent solution that manages to combine more modern social network features in an effort to provide for efficient reporting of hazardous situation.

Recent Security Projects that are funded by the European Union under the HORIZON 2020 program aim, also, to enhance the role of community policing. To achieve this, some of them decided to develop a mobile application for two-way communication. INSPEC2T (INSPEC2T Project 2017) targets to develop a specific application for dissemination and gathering of real time information from the police to the citizens and vice versa. CITYCOP (CITYCOP Project 2017) is another project that has the similar scope and aims to create a system of combination of mobile application and on-line portal. On the other hand, UNITY (UNITY Project 2017) is a project that aims to develop and provide a community policing model in which citizens and police will have an effective and practical cooperation, based on the development of a communications technology.

GDPR and Mobile Applications

Internet connectivity in recent years is characterized by "3E" (Everywhere, Every-time, Everything). That means that people are willing to connect to the Internet from everywhere (home, work, entertainment etc.), at every-time (working days, weekends, day, night etc.), with every-thing (pc, tablets, smartphones, smart TVs, wearables etc.). The daily necessity for Internet connectivity is accompanied by an increasing demand for applications in order to cover all aspects of user's needs. Thus, millions of applications are available online, the majority of them requires access to data stored in user's devices. The data stored to user's devices usually are correlated with user information such as name, age, gender, location and several other personal information.

Millions of mobile applications are available from several online web-stores, while the relevant market is characterized by duopoly since the two main players, Google Play and Apple Store, have a large portion of the market in terms of mobile apps availability.

In Google Play store the available mobile apps are provided either free of charge or paid and are organized in several categories. In each category, mobile apps are further grouped by Google taking into account the popularity, the date of release, or user preferences. In (Polykalas et al. 2017) researchers analyzed a sample of the most popular, free of charge, mobile apps provided by Google Play store, in order to examine the type as well as the extent of personal data access required by mobile apps. It was found that the majority of the examined mobile apps (84%) require

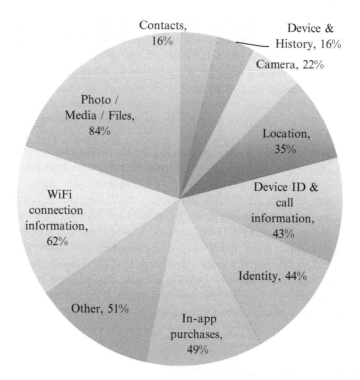

Fig. 7.1 Required access type by mobile apps

access to the data type "Photo/Media/File", while more than half of the examined mobile apps require access to "Wi-Fi connection information" (62%). "In apps purchases", "Identify" and "Device ID & call information" type of access follow with 49%, 44% and 43% percentage of the examined mobile apps, respectively Fig. 7.1.

For users who are willing to get more informed about the types of access, Google provides a short description of each type of access. For the most popular type (Photo/Media/File) is mentioned that: "*An app can use files or data stored on your device. Photos/Media/Files access may include the ability to: Read the contents of your USB storage (example: SD card), Modify or delete the contents of your USB storage, Format external storage, Mount or unmount external storage*". In practice this type of access, allows mobile apps to get access to almost all files or data stored in user's devices, while overlaps several other categories, explaining in such a way, the high popularity of this type of access among the rest types. Adopting the assumption that the sample of the examined mobile apps (10 most popular apps in each category – total 529 examined apps) is representative of all mobile apps available in Google Play store, it could be argued that there are more than 2.2 million of apps in Google Play store, which require access to almost all files stored in user's personal devices.

The rapid increase of online connected personal devices has brought new challenges to policy makers in relation to the protection of personal data. To this content a new Regulation was approved and published by European Parliament, aiming to the protection of EU citizens' personal data from unlawful collection, storage and processing of personal data. In (Spyros 2017) the new framework laid down by the Regulation is discussed giving emphasis to the procedures that an online mobile app store or/and a mobile app developer, should follow in case that the provision of a service/application, requires personal data storage/collection/processing. The Regulation imposes as a fundamental precondition for any personal data process the existence of user consent. In addition, two basic principles are imposed in relation to personal data privacy: the data minimization and purpose limitation. Data minimization refers to the correlation between the extent of personal data collection/processing and the purpose for which are collected. Purpose limitation refers to the transparent and explicit determination of purposes in which personal data are collected/stored/processed. Last but not least, the Regulation introduces more strictly rules in cases of minor users. In particular, if users are under 16-year-old then the process of personal data is lawful only to the extent that the person who has the responsibility of the minor has given his/her consent for the processing of minor's personal data.

Coming back to the discussion in relation to the current procedures followed in Google Play store and taking into account the main principles introduced by the GDPR several inconsistences could be highlighted. First of all, it could be argued that, the current procedures are not in compliance with the two main principles of Regulation regarding data minimization and purpose limitation. In particular, as discussed earlier, the majority of mobile apps require access to almost all files stored in user devices without an appropriate justification regarding the necessity of this type of access. In addition, it is not clear the correlation between the purpose of personal data collection and the extent of personal data access. Furthermore, the current procedures are not in compliances with the new rules in relation to minor protection. More specific a user under 16 is currently able to download and install in his/her personal device a mobile app, which require access to minor personal data without the consent of the person who has the responsibility of the minor.

TRILLION Mobile Applications

With TRILLION aiming to use state of the art technology to encourage the action of community policing, the use of mobile phones and wearables will play a very significant role in this effort. Location information, device info, access to media files and time-stamp of the data are some of the information that might be shared with when a TRILLION mobile application is used by a citizen or LEA. Taking under consideration, the sensitive and personal nature of these data, TRILLION's performance will be highly affected by the new European GDPR.

In TRILLION, each user in order to enter in the application should register with his/her credentials; therefore, an account should be created. The reason is both for feedback on the status of a submitted report directly to the interested user, but also to avoid any false alerts by identifying users that are misleading the LEAs. In addition, TRILLION will support hidden identity reporting by using a special architecture that manages to hide the user identity if he/she selects this kind of communication with the LEAs, providing also end-to-end encryption to increase the security of that communication. To achieve this, the TRILLION platform architecture will include a two-step anonymization process, which is described in (Chatzigeorgiou et al. 2017) in more detail.

On top of this, TRILLION will allow the users to send media files attached with their reports. The user will be allowed to select what should be included in their report and, apart from a short text description of the event there is no obligation as to including any attachments and/or upload a media file. As a further privacy enhancement, photos that will be taken from the application to be attached in a report (an option that will prompt the users to access the camera and take a photo will be included) will not be included in the phone's gallery and, therefore, if the phone falls in the hands of a malicious user, then he/she will not have access to them.

But for TRILLION to work efficiently and according to the regulation, detailed descriptions and/or instructions as to the reason the applications needs to access specific sensors and data should be provided to the users. Prompt messages should also be included to ask for explicit access to specific sensors and their generated data, e.g., the camera or the GPS signal of the smartphone. Those requests should be followed by details about how these data will be processed by TRILLION, in an effort to help for the efficient and smooth operation of the system, but, also, to encourage the user to permit the access. Furthermore, the user should be given the opportunity to query about and verifying that the data have been used for the described purpose and report if something is not working as it is supposed to. The above described functionality, designed for TRILLION's mobile applications, shows that they can comply with the lawfulness, fairness and transparency, data minimization and purpose limitation principles described in the GPDR and will allow them to work efficiently under the upcoming changes in the regulation.

On the other hand, as far as the protection of minors is concerned TRILLION demands the user to specify his/her age during the registration in the system, but up until now, no specific mechanisms have been adopted based on the received information.

Conclusions

In this paper, we investigated the compliance of the GDPR with the mobile applications in Google Play, in an effort to check the readiness of the today digital era and that of the IoT ecosystem with the changes that are described in GDPR. We have found that the majority of applications will not comply with the strict requirements of the GDPR, showcasing a large security gap in the existing regulation. Also, by using TRILLION as a use-case, we presented the mobile applications designed for it and their compliance to the new regulation. The results have shown that following the security by design technique can lead to create applications that can comply, in a very large degree, with the new European data protection regulation and, at the same time, achieve the necessary operations to perform efficiently and with great results.

Acknowledgements This work is funded by the European Commission under grant number H2020-FCT-2014, REA grant agreement n° [653256]. The support is gratefully acknowledged.

References

Chatzigeorgiou, C., Toumanidis, L., Kogias, D., Patrikakis, C., & Jacksch, E. (2017). A communication gateway architecture for ensuring privacy and confidentiality in incident reporting", in the 1st International Workshop on the Internet of People and Things (IPAT 2017), June 7–9, London, 2017.

CITYCOP Project, HORIZON 2020, https://www.citycop.eu/. Last accessed at September 2017.

INSPEC2T Project, HORIZON 2020, http://inspec2t-project.eu/en/the-project-2. Last accessed at September 2017.

NEXTDOOR. (n.d.). The private social network for your neighborhood. http://nextdoor.com

Polykalas, S. E., Prezerakos, G. N., Chrysidou, F. D., & Pylarinou, E. D. (2017). Mobile apps and data privacy: when the service is free, the product is your data, In proceedings of IEEE/IISA 2017, August 2017, Larnaca Cyprus.

Spyros, E. (2017). Polykalas, assessing EU framework for personal data privacy: Is the end of "take it or leave it" approach for downloading apps?, in proceedings of 7th international conference on social media technologies, communication, and informatics, October 2017, Athens Greece.

TRILLION Project, HORIZON 2020, http://trillion-project.eng.it/#/. Last accessed at July 2017.

UNITY Project, HORIZON 2020, https://www.unity-project.eu/. Last accessed at September 2017.

Xpose. (n.d.). https://xpose.tv/howitworks

Open Access This chapter is licensed under the terms of the Creative Commons Attribution 4.0 International License (http://creativecommons.org/licenses/by/4.0/), which permits use, sharing, adaptation, distribution and reproduction in any medium or format, as long as you give appropriate credit to the original author(s) and the source, provide a link to the Creative Commons license and indicate if changes were made.

The images or other third party material in this chapter are included in the chapter's Creative Commons license, unless indicated otherwise in a credit line to the material. If material is not included in the chapter's Creative Commons license and your intended use is not permitted by statutory regulation or exceeds the permitted use, you will need to obtain permission directly from the copyright holder.

Chapter 8
ICTs and Community Policing: An Ethical Framework

G. Galdon Clavell, M. M. Zamorano, and J. M. Zavala Pérez

Measuring the impact of innovation in CP is a necessary action that ensures the achievement of beneficial outcomes, nourishing positive community-police relationships while minimizing negative externalities such as bias, discrimination or a negative impact on social cohesion. The present work aims at filling this gap through the construction of an ethical framework in this field based on both the results of desk research activities and empirical fieldwork. The first provide an ethical framework for technology-mediated community policing by identifying, compiling and analysing preceding cases, successes and failures, and key factors to be considered. The second sheds light on specific ethical considerations and socio-cultural settings.

Impacts of Innovation in Community Policing

This section explores both the positive and the negative aspects of technology-mediated community policing by evaluating societal and ethical aspects. Paying attention to societal and ethical issues helps to prevent negative or unintended consequences that could worsen police-community relationships, further communities' distrust towards the police, create information overflow or too much responsibility for individual officers, and lead to calumny and defamation of innocents.

Through information technology, people can make their voices heard and communicate their concerns to the police effectively; at the same time, the police can use these media to identify the specific demands of any given community and the causes of their feelings of insecurity. Further, they can also employ crowdsourcing

G. Galdon Clavell (✉) · M. M. Zamorano · J. M. Zavala Pérez
Eticas Research & Consulting, Barcelona, Spain
e-mail: gemma@eticasconsulting.com

© The Author(s) 2018
G. Leventakis, M. R. Haberfeld (eds.), *Societal Implications of Community-Oriented Policing and Technology*, SpringerBriefs in Criminology,
https://doi.org/10.1007/978-3-319-89297-9_8

techniques to gather information about crimes, crime patterns and other hazards, and effectively respond to those. Additionally, social media channels can help the police to inform the public and make its work more transparent and relatable. In turn, ICTs can help establish better police accountability as the public can employ media channels for 'policing the police' and communicating cases of police abuse.

However, the use of ICTs can also be source of negative and undesirable effects. First of all, the extensive use of modern technology can lead to policing strategies that benefit certain groups and disadvantage others, as digital literacy and access to technology is not equally distributed within a society and varies according to age, wealth, social class and other factors. Moreover, crowdsourcing information from the public can lead to the spread of false rumours and accusations, and civil initiatives can even lead to cases of unlawful lynch mob justice. When employing statistical data and data correlations and extensive means of surveillance, technology-mediated community policing can potentially foster racial profiling and discrimination against minorities and reinforce stereotypes. Further, if data and statistics are employed for predictive policing, and if police action is fostered by assumptions based on past correlations, this can transgress the presumption of innocence to which democratically justified policing is bound. Therefore, it is important to keep fundamental rights and their protection in mind, such as the right to privacy, the right to informative self-determination, the right to physical and mental integrity, freedom of expression and presumption of innocence.

ICTs and Policing

In policing contexts, information and communication technologies (ICTs) have many different applications and uses. In many cases, police may utilize the standard privately-owned social media platforms and their services, such as *Twitter*, *Facebook*, *WhatsApp* and *YouTube*. These can be employed to foster a good relationship between the community and the police but also to make police work more relatable and transparent by communicating about everyday activities. For instance, the American Civil Liberties Union has released the freeware app *Police Tape*, which allows civilians to record law enforcement encounters.

Many of the 'standard' social platforms and their functionalities are often employed not only in emergencies and daily police work, but also by (para)policing initiatives that originate from civil society itself. Examples of such initiatives are so-called *neighbourhood watch (NW)* initiatives, which may have different degrees of authorization and official recognition, varying from country to country. They describe civil initiatives in which citizens organize and take action to help each other and foster community relations, but also to prevent crime and increase safety in their neighbourhoods. In the US, Los Angeles' so-called *Large Emergency Event Digital Information Repository*, or short LEEDIR,[1] is an "eyewitness platform",

---

[1] LEEDIR website: http://www.leedir.com

where citizens upload files or broadcast their webcams to share photos and videos of crime scenes, incidents, or other material they find important to share with the police during large scale events, attacks, disasters and so forth. They can also integrate external content from services like *Facebook*, *Google*, *Instagram* and *YouTube* for this purpose.

TapShield is another app related to 'crowd-sourced' policing. TapShield's aim is to empower citizens to feel safer, especially when walking the streets at night, by being directly and continuously connected to the police or others via their phone, and by using community-based security through crowd-sourced information about incidents. It makes extensive use of GPS tracking and includes functions like a silent alarm that can be used to inform the police of an emergency or attack discreetly and without the knowledge of the perpetrators; alerts about crime incidents around its user's location; a one-key function for phoning the police; an alarm which can be sent when headphones are removed; and a way for pedestrians to share their route and estimated time of arrival with their family or friends.[2] This app also uses crowdsourcing techniques to match up reported incidents with maps and the GPS coordinates of users. Matching up of crime data with geolocation data is a widely employed way to use ICTs for policing purposes; the resulting maps are called *crime maps*.

Community Policing Failures

If the societal and ethical implications of technology-mediated policing practices are not given enough consideration in advance, undesired consequences may occur.

In 2014, the New York Police Department (NYPD) launched the #myNYPD Twitter campaign[3] and asked people to tweet photos with members of the department under that hashtag. The social media campaign was meant to shed a positive light on the work of the department and its officers in the city. However, contrary to NYPD's expectations, people started using the promoted hashtag to tweet and share pictures of police brutality and abuse in the city, mocking NYPD's social media effort (Tran 2014). The department could have anticipated that people would use the platform and take up the hashtag to make their frustration heard. Such sharing systems are good for enabling people to perform 'sousveillance' on their authorities and hence increase police accountability, but at the same time they may foster a negative image of them.

Other unexpected and undesirable effects were also observable during the Boston Marathon Bombing. When the police started to crowd-source information, this apparently also invited civil 'internet detectives' to start a downright manhunt by making speculative claims on the basis of their personal analyses of pictures on the web. These claims consequently led to a number of false accusations that had severe

---

[2] TAPSHIELD website: http://TapShield.com/works

[3] Twitter (#mynypd): https://twitter.com/hashtag/mynypd

repercussions for their victims, who received threats and insults. Such developments emphasize the need to always weigh potential gains from crowdsourcing police work against the potential harm this can cause. Police forces have to develop reliable mechanisms to ensure that information is communicated as accurately and comprehensively as possible, and that inaccurate accusations or rumours are dismantled in real time.

When it comes to societal and ethical aspects of community policing, issues of social justice such as racial profiling, the perpetuation of prejudices and discrimination against minorities present a major factor. The introduction of ICTs does not ensure that bad practices will be avoided. On the contrary, technologies themselves may incorporate and remark biases. The iPhone app *SketchFactor* for example has been criticized from a social justice perspective. It was designed to let people crowd-source and share information about the "sketchiness" of neighbourhoods and report on people they deem suspicious or dangerous. This app has been criticized for perpetuating racism and discrimination, as it appears to facilitate the spread of stereotypes and labelling neighbourhoods based on subjective impressions and opinions (Biddle 2014). Since the app's crime maps are based on opinion more than on evidence, its data is inaccurate and its crime reports do not match up with the police's official crime maps. *SketchFactor* reports are not reviewed before they become visible to everyone, and they can be quite biased or vague in tone. For the same reasons, Microsoft's *Pedestrian Route Production* app, which offers similar functions, has been viewed critically and consequently been dubbed the "Avoid Ghetto" app (King 2012).

Risks and Societal Impact of ICTs

There is a set of aspects related to policing activity where the ICTs may have both a potential positive and negative impact. Among them: the performance of the interventions; the crime prevention plans; the effectiveness of communication; the social engagement and social cohesion; the trust towards authorities and within communities, and the public image of police forces.

The prevention and mitigation of potential risks that may appear during the implementation of ICT-based CP projects must consider a wide range of factors. All the stakeholders, including officers, victims, suspects, witnesses, etc., must play a role in the design and assessment phases. Personal safety during crow-sourced actions is also a key question to be included in the planning: involved citizens must not be put at risk and their contribution must be limited to safe activities (e.g. information). The conjunction of ICTs and security also raises obvious concerns on risks regarding increased surveillance threatened privacy guarantees. Management of information is another crucial aspect to be considered during the risk assessment: misinformation, rumours, false accusations and uncontrolled data are potential consequences that would affect the desirability of a system. Usability problems are also to be controlled, including digital divide and unequal access to the developed technologies, which may question the actual contribution and shared benefits of the project. Lastly, risks include unlawful practices and biased interventions based on profiling and discrimination.

Measuring the Impact: Analysis and Assessment

In order to avoid such negative effects, the employment of ICTs in community policing requires a thorough analysis of its ethical and societal implications, which should build the basis for the establishment of solid guidelines and policies to follow. Further, such an analysis can inform the value-sensitive design of technologies for policing purposes. If information technologies are employed, data management strategies need to be created in order to mitigate potential risks. A multi-step approach, that intervenes before, during and after the implementation of the innovations improves the chances for a successful and effective assessment. The prior evaluation should take place during the design of the tool or service and must take into account the legal framework, the State of the art, the specific context and potential existing incompatibilities. The assessment of the work in progress must consider the potential effects of the chosen elements and functionalities, the evaluation of the demonstrations/tests and suggest the necessary corrections. The **final evaluation and oversight** entails the evaluation of the final product and a periodic replicable assessment (e.g. a checklist), measuring the effects on the long term, detecting needs for updates and predicting the chances for sustainability.

Contextual, Human and Technological Factors in Community Policing

Any general discussion of societal and ethical aspects can only function as a guideline for thinking through potential risks and applications, but the concrete framework will have to be adjusted case by case – there is no single model that suits all ICT-mediated CP initiatives. Community policing always deals with and responds to contextually unique situations. The following section provides an overview of different contextual factors, such as issues of prejudice, discrimination and social justice, police integrity and accountability, digital divides and data handling. The specific socio-cultural setting in which a practice is implemented, the community's particular social structure, the neighbourhood's history and its existing community-police relations all shape the way community policing is carried out, its societal effects and its overall success. The success and desirability of CP practices varies from country to country. However, we can suspect differences in attitudes toward community policing and neighbourhood watch initiatives between different groups of a country's inhomogeneous population.

For CP initiatives it can be important to employ officers who are thoroughly familiar with the community, its people and culture, due to their knowledge and understanding of the community, which is needed to make the right contextual decisions. However, employing local officers it not necessarily a guarantee for desired outcomes like good community-police relations (Ziembo-Vogl and Meško 2000). In the case of the "dirty 30", a group of local CP officers in the NYPD had used their position and their good connections within the community to participate in and eventually profit from major drug deals in the community for 3 years. The distributed character of community policing and its flat hierarchies can sometimes complicate oversight of police activities. CP officers carry higher responsibility as they have to make decisions more autonomously, but this also diminishes accountability and oversight. An app like *CrimePad*, which makes it possible for police on the beat to document incidents, share information and get advice from other officers in real time, can hence offer support and help establish better oversight (Byrne 2014).

The efficacy of social media campaigns will also depend on the profile of its target audience, which could imply that different strategies would be required. The digital divide, which describes inequalities in the use and access to modern ICTs could play a key role (Van Dijk 2006). Due to this factor, the use of ICTs in policing might create a social bias or discriminate against certain people (elderly, low-income, disabled, etc.), implying different chances to benefit from public security innovations. Therefore, different degrees of technological literacy have to be taken into account: for instance, the *SketchFactor* app, has been criticized for being available only for iPhones and not for cheaper devices (Cueto 2014).

The reliability of crowd-sourced information is another great challenge. A reliable system has to be based on data that surpassed the problem of information quality, which means that it complies with certain requisites in terms of relevance, quantity, accuracy, timeliness, completeness, format and availability (Bharosa et al. 2009). There have been numerous cases where people have sabotaged initiatives, uploaded fake or manipulated images, or consciously spread false information. For this reason, some projects have worked on creating technologies that allow the verification of the origin and date of a picture, or other image-related data.[4] In addition to ensuring data reliability, it is important to secure the stored records properly, so vulnerable information is protected from being hacked and manipulated.

Community Policing is linked to the problem-oriented policing approach, which focuses on the systematic causes for certain crime patterns; this approach defends that it is better to tackle the root of the problem and prevent crimes *before* they happen. Predictive policing is based on this premise, and uses surveillance and data collection to statistically analyse crime patterns and to introduce measures aimed at reducing those factors leading to criminal activity. Nevertheless, this approach may foster conflicts with the right to presumption of innocence. Predictions always depend on likelihood and can never be 100% certain; additionally they are often biased by prejudices or can perpetuate negative stereotypes. Hence, it can be ques-

---

[4] Stopfake.org: *13 online tools that help to verify the authenticity of a photo.* http://www.stopfake.org/en/13-online-tools-that-help-to-verify-the-authenticity-of-a-photo/

tionable to employ data for 'precrime' efforts, both with regard to our obligation to presume innocence and because relying on statistics can stigmatize innocent people and law-abiding citizens just because they belong to a certain group, such as immigrants or minorities.

Ethical Framework for ICT-Mediated Community Policing

In order to appraise the societal aspects of technology-mediated community policing it is important to focus on their broad scope of applications, whereas the societal impact of technological developments can be explored according to four sub-dimensions (Fig. 8.1): desirability (the actual need of a certain technology), acceptability (the extent to which a technological innovation will be welcomed by a community), ethics (the shared values and moral standards embedded in a society) and data management (the consequences a system may have regarding privacy and data protection).

The present results are based on a research that took place in the context of the INSPEC²T project (Inspiring CitizeNS Participation for Enhanced Community PoliCing AcTions). This initiative, funded by the European Commission under the

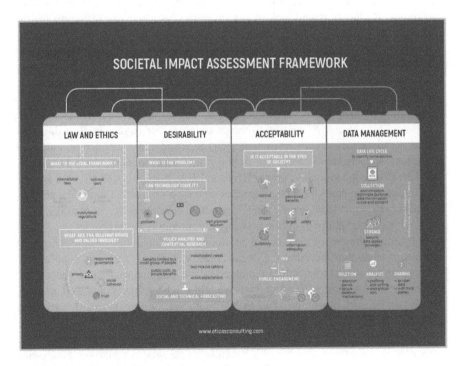

Fig. 8.1 Four-tier societal impact assessment framework

H2020-FCT-2014 call, aims at developing a sustainable framework for Community Policing that effectively addresses and promotes seamless collaboration between the police and the community, for which it will deliver a real time two-way communication platform for citizens and police.

A total of 12 focus groups, 6 with LEAs and 6 with citizens, were conducted in 6 European cities, each one having one of each. By having a wide diversity of participants in both cases, recruiters minimized several factors that could have biased the discussion such as age, rank, years of experience and division for LEAs whereas for citizens background, age, sex and previous knowledge of CP programs. The cities where fieldwork was conducted were Athens (Greece), Belfast (UK), Nicosia (Cyprus) Groningen (the Netherlands), Preston, UK and Valencia (Spain).

Around the dimension of 'desirability', the participants gave a positive feedback: they highlighted that CP officers were 'part of the community', valued positively the face to face contact, and the closeness to the citizens. The consensus around the concept of community policing was focus on crime prevention, which was achieved through mechanisms like meetings, talks, and mediation. This allows them to gather intelligence that can prove to be useful for prevention as it allows the LEA to monitor real or potential conflicts and act accordingly before crime takes place. Furthermore, this information can also be used for mediation purposes, something which is fundamental in CP programs. Nevertheless, LEAs have had to adapt to new challenges and feel it has been themselves as individuals rather than the institutions who have had to keep up with the changes in an environment of growing financial constraints. Budget cuts and lack of resources has been a major difficulty for the effective application of CP programs.

Regarding the 'acceptability' axis, CP programs have been positively reviewed by the citizens. Many participants can recall a case where CP has been effective, and value highly its deterrent effect. There is also general awareness of successful mediation programs run by the police. By and large CP has had good effects in conflicting neighbourhoods whenever implemented, despite the budget cuts of which citizens are also aware. According to the participants, the engagement of the community is satisfactory except for certain age groups and minorities. Even though CP programms may benefit both police organizations and citizenry, the results show that there is no educational program offered to LEAs that covers all relevant aspects to CP. Some participants have taken courses on their own which address the particular skillset and knowledge needed in CP which may range from psychology, communication or mediation, to public housing or community management.

The 'ethics' dimension reveals that community building relies on defending a set of shared values that facilitate the coexistence. Resilience, trust and a culture of cooperation are some of the values remarked by the participants. Citizens admit that many times it is the community itself who requires to be properly educated and they demand an education program, run by the municipality, which would work both ways, thus creating clusters of citizens that can help as observants for the police and holding regular meetings where there would be an exchange of information. All LEA groups remark the absence of a concrete framework in which CP duties take place. There are some guidelines that may be established occasionally according to the ward/area, but from the institution standpoint, the line between CP and normal policing is today rather blurry. With regard to citizens' participation, this issue prompted many doubts and questions amongst those participants less acquainted with CP and those who show general criticism towards the police force. They stress the importance of anonymity when contacting the police as it is crucial avoiding the idea of "snitching". Participants understand there is a lot of work to do on the part of authorities and political powers in order to create, first, a logical framework in which CP activities can be undertaken, and second, a culture of cooperation amongst police professionals and citizens alike.

Concerning 'data management', there is a lot of confusion and lack of information as to how data is, can or should be managed. On the one hand all participants understand that technology is developing at an ever faster pace and they need to keep up with it. In their view, ICT innovations offer virtually limitless real and potential solutions, but they admit there are many grey areas in terms of usability and privacy. All LEA focus groups demand more technical support and better management with regards to technological platforms which would allow real-time contact between LEAs and citizens. Issues like data protection and privacy raise many doubts amongst participants, especially questions related to uses of phone-taken images as evidence, anonymity of informants or use of social media. LEAs adopt a broad common sense stance towards these issue. Citizens demands and expectations revolve around the problem of oversight and ethics, more specifically, questioning who manages the data and what will they do with it. They state that in an ideal world citizens should not have any problem when sharing information with the police, but they are aware that the system does not function at its best as of yet, which adds up to certain general confusion as to how new technologies are bringing about issues related to privacy. Increasing concerns are related to the fact that new technologies provide a wider range of means for the management of documentation, like evidences, in different multimedia formats (video, pictures, audio, text, etc.). The management of virtual communities and social media accounts are also concerning questions, and citizens have also raised some concerns regarding the potential increase of surveillance. A last topic is the ownership of the used devices, and the potential utilization of own devices (e.g. mobile phones or social media accounts).

Conclusions and Recommendations

Community policing is seen as an effective means of policing in the context of growing diversity in communities and less resources for public services. Technology and community collaboration can overcome the constraints of less agents on the ground. Nevertheless, these initiatives have to work in building mutual trust between community and police forces. Education and communication are key factors, and youngsters are a key social group that has to be reached if the service is to be successful. Technology raises a lot of expectations to balance the lack of resources. However, it generates certain confusion as participants feel it moves at a fast pace difficult to keep up with, which raises some new challenges related to privacy and fundamental rights amongst citizens. In order to ensure a successful implementation of ICT-mediated community policing resources, the following aspects are to be taken into account.

Relevance

Clear needs, goals and demands have to be detected. The resulting tool should be able to channelize the actual safety needs and demands of the benefited communities, in order to jointly define relevant and broad-embracing safety strategies. These needs, goals and demands define the functionalities of the resulting tools and thus, the proportional and relevant balance between benefits and drawbacks, risks and opportunities. The decision-making procedures in the project should reflect the idea that technology is a means, not a goal itself.

Empowerment

In order to comply with the participative nature of CP, the preferences of both LEAs and citizenry have to be taken into account. The effective empowerment of citizens, both as individuals but also as members of the existing communities (emphasizing them as a plurality of groups) should encourage their active engagement into the social structures and networks. Moreover, the benefits have to be equally distributed, and not being concentrated by specific groups (e.g. specific end-users, privileged communities, providers and developers).

Stakeholders

A wide scope of stakeholders has to be considered in order to address a community integrally: different types of LEAs at different levels of the command chain (CP officers, patrol unit officers, etc.); policymakers and civil servants; social workers; members of the public (community leaders and mediators, young people and elderly people, housewives/men, repeat offenders...); involved industry members (technology and telecommunications providers).

Context

It is important to bear in mind the spatial and temporal conditions that will affect the functioning of the system. The scalability and modularity depicted in the theoretical design has to be concordant with the actual time and place where the tools are to be deployed. Different administrative levels may be implied and the limits of interoperability (especially regarding the sharing of data) have to be defined and respected. On the other hand, it has to be conveniently studied to which extent the online/virtual communities play a meaningful role in the project.

Trust

Democratic values as transparency and accountability as well as the corresponding oversight mechanisms should not be seen as trade-offs or obstacles for an effective policing strategy. Trust is a key value that should be conceived as a goal itself, and not just as a means to achieve the active collaboration of citizens. Damaged trust between citizens and police, inside a specific community, or between different communities/neighbourhoods may even initiate additional security problems and conflicts. Individualist attitudes derived from this damage erode the social tissue sustained by the communities.

Agency and Participation

Differing involvement levels available for citizenry may co-exist. Yet undesired or involuntary involvement is strongly discouraged. Moreover, different engagement levels should not imply individual nor social benefits (beyond the satisfaction of the participation and collaboration) or disadvantages. The undesired involvement can occur in a subtle way, since crowd-sourced tasks may be ineffective: defamation and false accusations are a major risk in this sense. Both victims' and offenders' information has to be respectfully managed, but also unconnected citizens should have the option to remain unaffected.

Safety First

Even though citizens are asked to collaborate and to some extent, they are legally obliged to do so, the involvement of citizens in security tasks has to be limited. Otherwise, disproportionate risks could be assumed by community members that are not prepared or legally entitled for certain high risk actions or involvements (violence utilization, investigative actions, etc.). Injuries, threats and even death are plausible risks related to the inadequate understanding of the integration of citizens into security contexts.

Anonymity

The anonymous interaction through ICTs should not be perceived as a drawback. Moreover, it could make people more willing to participate and collaborate. Anonymity of both the informing party and the affected party has to be respected, as well as the identity of police officers out of the policing context. Conditioning the utilization of a tool to the revelation of personal data (e.g. geolocalization) has to be justified, in the sense that the functionalities demand it as an unavoidable requirement. The risk of misuse like providing false hints, if conveniently managed, may be minor than the consequences of processing personal data that is not essential for the effective functioning of a tool.

Social Media

Responsible stakeholders have to be aware of the types of information circulating, which has to be relevant to the needs, goals and demands, as well as compliant to the legal framework. Through social media environments, police forces may post and circulate awareness-oriented information (i.e., security-related social media information) which can be managed by both LEAs and internet users; but hey may also perform social media crawling and reutilize the information found. Circulating other persons' contents may endanger data protection rights and copyright, and it could end up circulating false facts and rumours. For this reason, social media reutilization of other's contents by both LEAs and citizens has to be carried out with precaution or directly avoided.

Accesibility

Usability and simplicity of functions help to achieve the relevant goals as well as to compensate for the regulation complexity. Technology has not to be developed for the sake of technology, just due to the availability of options and resources. Different access to knowledge and to technological resources should not be translated into different access to security and participation. Discrimination may occur if these questions are not taken into account: digital divides, cultural and social aspects (e.g. languages), unavailability for disabled people, etc.

Resources

Any ICT-based tool must ensure the long-term sustainability and maintenance. Allocating the necessary resources is a key requirement for the success of the resulting tools. Additionally, officers should have the convenient material and cognitive resources in order to be able to respond to the different situations, without having to make use of their own private means. Past experiences reveal that efforts for the introduction of innovative technologies in policing may be unsuccessful if they are not also supported by an adequate follow-up plan. Especially important is the training of staff upon a wide perspective: not only regarding the utilization of technologies but also acquiring behavioural patterns (e.g. by codes of conduct) that allow to take advantage of the tools at the most. This knowledge has to be transferable, adaptable and understandable.

References

Bharosa, N., Appelman, J., van Zanten, B., & Zuurmond, A. (2009). Identifying and confirming information and system quality requirements for multi-agency disaster management. In J. Landgren & S. J. Gothenburg (Eds.), *Proceedings of the 6th International ISCRAM Conference,* Sweden, May 2009.

Biddle, S. (2014). Smiling young white people make app for avoiding black neighborhoods. Valley WAG, July 8. http://valleywag.gawker.com/smiling-young-white-people-make-app-for-avoiding-black-1617775138. Accessed 25 Mar 2016.

Byrne, C. (2014). How an iPad app is transforming the way police work crime scenes. Fast Company – Co.Labs, January 22. http://www.fastcolabs.com/3025289/how-an-ipad-app-is-transforming-the-way-police-work-crime-scenes. Accessed 25 Mar 2016.

Cueto, E. (2014). Sketch factor app is racist — Not on purpose, but that Doesn't make it better. *Bustle,* August 8. http://www.bustle.com/articles/35065-sketch-factor-app-is-racist-not-on-purpose-but-that-doesnt-make-it-better. Accessed 25 Mar 2016.

Goode, E. (2011). Police lesson: Social network tools have two edges. *The NY Times,* April 6. http://www.nytimes.com/2011/04/07/us/07police.html?_r=0; http://www.theguardian.com/world/2014/apr/23/mynypd-twitter-call-out-new-york-police-backfires. Accessed 25 Mar 2016.

King, J. (2012). Why Microsoft's So-Called 'Avoid Ghetto' App Is Really American. *Color Lines,* January 31. http://www.colorlines.com/articles/why-microsofts-so-called-avoid-ghetto-app-really-american. Accessed 25 Mar 2016.

Tran, M. (2014). #myNYPD Twitter callout backfires for New York police department. *The Guardian,* April 23. Accessed 25 Mar 2016.

Van Dijk, J. A. (2006). Digital divide research, achievements and shortcomings. *Poetics, 34*(4), 221–235.

Ziembo-Vogl, J., & Meško, G. (2000). Conceptualizing the ethical aspects of community policing inception and practice. In M. Pagon (Ed.), *Policing in central and Eastern Europe: Ethics, integrity and human rights* (pp. 523–536). Ljubljana: College of Police and Security Studies.

Open Access This chapter is licensed under the terms of the Creative Commons Attribution 4.0 International License (http://creativecommons.org/licenses/by/4.0/), which permits use, sharing, adaptation, distribution and reproduction in any medium or format, as long as you give appropriate credit to the original author(s) and the source, provide a link to the Creative Commons license and indicate if changes were made.

The images or other third party material in this chapter are included in the chapter's Creative Commons license, unless indicated otherwise in a credit line to the material. If material is not included in the chapter's Creative Commons license and your intended use is not permitted by statutory regulation or exceeds the permitted use, you will need to obtain permission directly from the copyright holder.

Chapter 9
Project Genesis: A Strategic Review of Neighbourhood Policing in Dorset

Johannes Pieter Oosthuizen and Alison Wakefield

Introduction

Neighbourhood Policing Teams (NPTs) were introduced into Dorset in 2006 and neighbourhoods and boundaries were clearly defined through consultation with partners and communities (HMIC 2008). Dorset Police invested heavily in the creation of these NPTs across the county, but as Police Forces across England & Wales attempted to deliver their response to public austerity measures from 2010 by introducing change programmes, it is not surprising that these programmes planned to achieve most of their savings by reducing the number of police officers, Police Community Support Officers (PCSOs) and police staff. By August 2013, Dorset Police began to consider ways of improving their operational model of Neighbourhood Policing as they were entering a period of unprecedented challenge and this is when the review (Project Genesis) was initiated.

Methodology

The project adopted a mixed methods research strategy and the qualitative data was obtained from 18 semi-structured interviews with Neighbourhood Police Sergeants, together with three focus groups consisting of 19 police officers and

J. P. Oosthuizen (✉)
University of Winchester, Winchester, UK
e-mail: Johannes.Oosthuizen@winchester.ac.uk

A. Wakefield
University of Portsmouth, Portsmouth, UK

© The Author(s) 2018
G. Leventakis, M. R. Haberfeld (eds.), *Societal Implications of Community-Oriented Policing and Technology*, SpringerBriefs in Criminology,
https://doi.org/10.1007/978-3-319-89297-9_9

PCSOs. Electronic surveys were also distributed to 296 Neighbourhood Police Officers and staff from junior to senior ranks and produced an overall response rate of 59%. The quantitative data was taken from independent observational studies on 14 different NPTs in seven police stations on 62 different shifts over several months.

Operational Roles & Qualitative Data: Views from the Frontline

Dorset Police utilise three main roles in each of their operational NPTs, namely the Sergeant (supervisor and senior officer on each team), Police Constable and PCSO. Whilst there are additional supporting roles, the NPTs are the primary implementers of Neighbourhood Policing (NP) tactics and strategies within urban and rural areas throughout Dorset. When questioned about their operational procedures, over 77% (n14) of NPT sergeants stated that there was no adherence to organisational policies when dealing with problems in local communities, which allowed them to develop individualistic solutions. NP Constables were following the same approach and of the 94 PCs participating in the e-survey, 80% (n62) said that they developed their own bespoke and personalised solutions instead. A similar trend appeared with PCSOs, where 75% (n60) stated they adopted a similar approach in their roles. Whilst the utilisation of officer discretion is crucial within NP strategies, it is equally important to ensure that a corporate structure and framework exists within which that discretion may be utilised, to ensure that a strategic 'footprint' can clearly be seen in the application of policing responses to public concerns. This view is supported by Her Majesty's Inspectorate of Constabulary (HMIC) (College of Policing 2015), who stated that to effectively tackle public concerns and improve the quality of life in communities, police priorities, using their tasking and coordinating (TCG) process and supported by systems that monitor effectiveness and impact, must reflect the communities' concerns.

Structural Weaknesses

A review of Dorset Police's policies found that there were additional factors contributing toward a lack of organisational structure. The absence of a strategic focus appeared to be having a detrimental effect on the morale of officers in NPTs, particularly amongst front-line supervisors. When asked to describe the demands of public sector austerity and diminishing police budgets, 72% (n13) of NPT sergeants said the task was" difficult", "challenging", and" tough". One NPT supervisor who had 18 years' police experience and 7 years in Neighbourhood Policing, stated that "for the first time in my career, it has become difficult ..." (interviewee 3). Some interviewees went on to provide some examples, such as not having vehicle transport readily available (interviewee 7) and in some areas highlighting the case that only one NPT Constable was available for 12,000 residents (interviewee 9 & 10). The most frequent issue was that of diminishing NPT resources, where NPT officers were being abstracted on a regular basis into 24/7 patrol duties, to fill the gaps being created by a lack of recruitment. 62% (n66) of NP Constables stated they were being routinely detached from their NPT duties due to the Total Resource Management (TRM) policy[1], which was seen to be the greatest form of intrusion into their NPT roles. Over 50% of NPT sergeants felt that the future of NP in Dorset was directly linked to resources and one stated that "NP won't continue if our officers keep getting pulled back into patrol duties [interviewee 5]". Another supervisor suggested that "further losses of NPT officers will result in NP becoming a patrol function [interviewee 11]" and another warned that "our numbers will reduce and we will probably only be able to deliver lip-service [interviewee 16]".

Observational Studies: Examining the Data

NPTs should be responsible and accountable for levels of crime and Anti-Social Behaviour (ASB) in their geographic areas. This is not a new concept and many other forces do this already – recognising that all levels of crime take place in or affect people who live in neighbourhoods (Home Office 2004, p. 16). However, observational data from Project Genesis indicated that more than one third (37%) of NPT workloads were taken up with secondary tasks, such as administration, travel and custody-related issues and of the remaining 63%, only 8% was attributed to working with their local communities. Nearly 32% of NPT activity took place within police stations and only 11% of their tasks were associated with a specific set of criminal activities[2], of which 14% were with non-criminal/ASB/traffic work and 75% was associated with 'other' types of work, such as crime prevention patrol, reassurance, community meetings or activities specific to drugs, prostitution, etc. Unsurprisingly, PCSOs spent more time dealing with the public (67%) than PCs (58%).

Observational data showed that activities varied at each of the seven stations and an urban/rural split was apparent. Nearly 75% of activity was public facing

---

[1] Policy introduced by Dorset Police to move operational resources across the county, according to demand and need, when required. This frequently involved NPT officers being moved to patrol duties away from their geographical responsibilities.

[2] Violence, criminal damage, burglary and hate crime.

at rural stations, compared to 60% at urban and patrol activity was higher at rural stations (31%) than urban (20%). The biggest contrasts were observed in administrative tasks (3% for rural & 20% for urban - an observation in line with Dorset crime levels, which were consistently higher in urban areas): engaging local communities with collaborative problem-solving strategies was as low as 2% in some urban areas and 16% in rural stations (this highlighted significant weaknesses for NPTs in consulting and engaging the public, as well as attempting to involve local communities in resolving their own problems, particularly in urban areas).

Findings

Project Genesis produced a total of 44 recommendations and findings were divided into several key areas, such as detailing a precise understanding of the day-to-day operation of NP officers (measuring their activities around the detection, prevention and reduction of crime), how often supervisors, police officers and PCSOs were visible to the public, what strategies were being employed to engage local communities and what additional levels of training and knowledge were required to enhance their operational roles. The qualitative data highlighted how important it was that a coherent strategic concept of NP was understood corporately by managers and staff across all departments, to enable Neighbourhood police officers and PCSOs to provide a targeted and focused delivery. In addition, role profiles should be reviewed periodically, to ensure they are fit for purpose and avoid what is known as 'mission-creep'. Whilst the qualitative data revealed high levels of commitment in many of the officers, the data showed that NP officers only spend 26% of their time responding to incidents and 22% of their shift dealing with crime and ASB. These low levels of crime-based activities make it difficult for police officers to fully utilise their warranted powers and if they are to be more responsible and accountable for dealing with crime in their neighbourhoods, their role needs to be more targeted and specific.

Dorset Police has actively supported Neighbourhood Policing since 2006, but the lack of organisational review, training and modernisation has presented significant challenges for them and in September 2015, their Senior Command Team accepted all the recommendations of Project Genesis, introducing an amended model of Neighbourhood Policing for their 71 NPTs. An external validation of this process was recognised by the HMIC (2016), who stated that "the force has a well-established approach to evidence-based policing... The review [Project Genesis] of its neighbourhood policing function resulted in the adoption of best practice, improved services to the public and an increased understanding of communities".

References

College of Policing. (2015). *Delivering neighbourhood policing – A practice stocktake*. Coventry: College of Policing Limited.

HMIC. (2008, September 1). Her majesty's inspectorate of constabulary. Retrieved October 17, 2017, from HMIC Inspection Report: Dorset Police: Neighbourhood Policing: Developing Citizen Focus Policing: http://www.hmic.gov.uk/media/dorset-phase2-neighbourhood-policing-citizen-focus-20080830.pdf

HMIC. (2016). *PEEL: Police effectiveness 2015: An inspection of dorset police*. London: HMIC.

Home Office. (2004). *Building communities, beating crime: A better police service for the 21st century*. Norwich: The Stationery Office.

Open Access This chapter is licensed under the terms of the Creative Commons Attribution 4.0 International License (http://creativecommons.org/licenses/by/4.0/), which permits use, sharing, adaptation, distribution and reproduction in any medium or format, as long as you give appropriate credit to the original author(s) and the source, provide a link to the Creative Commons license and indicate if changes were made.

The images or other third party material in this chapter are included in the chapter's Creative Commons license, unless indicated otherwise in a credit line to the material. If material is not included in the chapter's Creative Commons license and your intended use is not permitted by statutory regulation or exceeds the permitted use, you will need to obtain permission directly from the copyright holder.

Chapter 10
1996 Initiatives to Integrate Technology into Community Oriented Policing – 20 Years Later

M. R. Haberfeld and Nickolaos Petropoulos

Introduction

The use of technology to improve community policing effectiveness has gained attention over the last decade, primarily due to the rise in the use of social media, however, it is far from new; back in 1996, at a time when the Web was still just a few years old, Google.com did not exist yet and there were only about 100,000 websites (in comparison to over a billion in 2014 (Lafrance 2015), the National Institute of Justice (NIJ) and the Office of Community Oriented Policing Services (COPS) organized a series of five regional conferences that focused on how technology can enhance community policing (NIJ 1996). The conferences were held in Colorado Springs, Colorado; Rochester, New York; San Diego, California; Charleston, South Carolina; and Louisville, Kentucky.

The overarching goal of the conferences was to search for and, eventually, identify ways in which technology could further enhance the relationship between law-enforcement and the community on a win-win basis. The attendees represented a diverse array of law enforcement professionals, including chiefs of various police departments across the country, government officials, consultants, managers, judges etc. and the vast majority of the presentations focused on how to identify meaningful ways to improve community policing through the use of technology. The thematic areas of the conferences included the following topics:

- Using the Internet for community policing purposes,
- How crime analysis technology can help mapping and tracking crime,
- Individual police department technology-facilitated strategies to fight crime,
- Various technology related liability considerations.

M. R. Haberfeld (✉) · N. Petropoulos
City University of New York, John Jay College of Criminal Justice, New York, NY, USA
e-mail: mhaberfeld@jjay.cuny.edu

© The Author(s) 2018
G. Leventakis, M. R. Haberfeld (eds.), *Societal Implications of Community-Oriented Policing and Technology*, SpringerBriefs in Criminology,
https://doi.org/10.1007/978-3-319-89297-9_10

It should also be noted that the conferences were organized 2 years after the establishment of the Office of Community Oriented Policing Services (COPS), as part of the 1994 Crime Act (Roth et al. 1994) through which the Congress was aiming to introduce technologies that would modernize policing. As a result, NIJ was heavily involved in the process and undertook the duty to build a vast and ambitious technology program that would include investments of assets and resources to assist police departments with more equipment, more training, and grants to purchase technology.

The presentations during the five conferences revolved around the use of technology for community policing purposes. A summary of the main points that were presented by both individual speakers and law-enforcement representatives follows below.

Ways in Which Technology Can Improve Community Policing Outreach and Effectiveness

Despite the dramatic increase of use of computers by law-enforcement agencies across the U.S., a 1993 Bureau of Justice Statistics survey revealed that only two-thirds of the Nation's 17,000 police departments were using computers in a consistent way on a daily basis (Northrop et al. 1995). These findings suggested that there is a serious need for police organizations to embrace technology in a more systematic and comprehensive way; COPS programs were aimed at helping law-enforcement agencies to achieve these goals, however, certain obstacles were identified that "impede the development of police technology" (NIJ 1996, p. 10). Those obstacles included the following:

- The fragmentation of police departments across the country that has made them either hard-to-reach markets for technology manufacturers or consumers with limited purchasing power due to lack of resources.
- Concerns over misuse of technology, both by police officers and the public. Those concerns include, but are not limited to, the notion of "big brother" surveillance systems that are employed by police departments to monitor their own officers' activities as well as citizens.

However, despite the above mentioned obstacles, the rapid growth of the Internet provides an array of opportunities for law enforcement agencies to use the Web in order to promote police-community relationships and collaboration. For example, the Internet could be used to inform the community of the latest crime trends or send out electronically, mainly via email, newsletters and other bits of information. Also, citizens could use the Internet to reach out to the local police forces with comments or concerns and get feedback. Also, training officers through the use of websites is another tool that could be used more in the future (NIJ 1996, p. 19). It was suggested that police departments should explore the possibility of creating their own websites.

Technology-Facilitated Community Policing Programs that Are Already Used by Police Departments Across the Country

Some model departments were featured as examples to a successful use of various technologies, among the Dallas Police Department, which introduced a number of tools to foster community policing effectiveness through the use of technology. Those tools included mobile neighbourhood police assistance centers, specially equipped vehicles that increased police mobility and allowed the officers to remain in a neighbourhood around the clock while delivering services to the community in crime-ridden areas. Another innovative tool used by Dallas P.D. was Fax Net, a crime prevention network that promoted the partnership between police and communities by alerting the latter of any criminal activity and wanted suspects in their area.

Another innovative approached from the District of Columbia Metropolitan Police Department included a state-of-the-art information management system that would allow officers to focus more on solving problems by spending more time with community members in the field rather than wasting time with other tasks. In order to achieve that, the department would implement the following three strategies "to use technology as a force multiplier" (NIJ 1996, p. 30):

- Assigning administrative work and duties to non-sworn personnel in order to give officers more time to engage with the community.
- Eliminate unnecessary work for patrol officers, mainly by using computer workstations and other technology to keep them more time in the field instead of the police station.
- Save money through the use of available technological tools and redirect the savings to solve more community problems.

The importance of tracking and mapping crime was highlighted in the case of the New York City Police Department's (NYPD) use of the GIS-based crime analysis; in the 1990's NYPD introduced new mapping and crime analysis program that allowed beat officers to have immediate and up-to-date access to data on crime patterns in their area through workstations connected to a local area network.(Goldsmith et al. 1999). At the time, this was an innovation that allowed precinct commander to become more effective in fighting crime. This effort was funded by the National Institute of Justice (NIJ) and was a collaboration between the NYPD and the Center for Urban Research and the Center for Applied Study of the Environment of the City University of New York, a unique partnership between law enforcement and academia in an effort to produce research that will facilitate the implementation of community policing interventions based on crime patterns and spatial analysis.

However, NYPD was not the only Department in the country that had introduced crime mapping technologies; Chicago Police Department developed an innovative crime analysis program, called Information Collection for Automated Mapping (ICAM) which was the first software in the American policing history developed "by police officers for police officers" (NIJ 1996, p. 47). What made this program unique was its design; it was built in a user-friendly way so that beat officers could use ICAM maps during community meetings in order to present and discuss with members of the community ways to address the crime-related problems of each neighbourhood. (Welch and Fulla 2005).

Other Crime-Detection Technologies

Detection of concealed weapons has been one of the major concern for law-enforcement agencies across the United States; the Departments of Defence and Justice collaborated in an effort to apply pre-existing technology used for military purposed to law enforcement settings. In particular, Rome Laboratories operating under the Defence Research Projects Agency (DAPRA) and the National Institute of Justice (NIJ) have focused on technologies that can assist police agencies to detect concealed weapons under problematic circumstances where visual detection is not possible, for example under heavy clothing. These technologies include infra-red imaging which detects the presence of a weapon "by showing its cooler image against the warmer body" (NIJ 1996, p. 72), acoustic imaging and X-ray imaging which can be used in controlled environments such as prisons. Although the use of concealed weapons detection technology for law-enforcement purposed was still relatively new, back in 1996, it appeared to be very promising and cost-effective.

Some Concerns Expressed by the Conference Attendees in 1996

One major observation noted was that police agencies need to be careful about the technologies they elect to use and that these innovations are not created in a vac-uum. One of the ideas presented suggested that the officers who will be eventually be asked to use the final product, for example, a sophisticated computer system, should participate actively in the design process. If the end-users needs, concerns and remarks are not taken into account during the preliminary stage of the imple-mentation of a technology, chances are that no matter how sophisticated this tech-nology or program is, its implementation will be problematic.

Another issue that was brought up during the conferences was that of constitution-related issues. Given that new technologies are an unchartered territory for law enforcement agencies, police departments should pay particular attention to liability and constitutional issues surrounding new technology and its implementation, including issues of privacy and civil rights protection. An effective approach to this issue could be the creation of working groups where law enforcement agents, pros-ecutors and academics would consider all the challenges posed by new technologies and come up with effective responses that would eliminate the challenges related to their implementation.

Although most experts in 1996 agreed that technology could boost the effectiveness of community policing, the major recommendation was police agencies should always consider three important rules when implementing community policing programs, namely right timing, possible resistance to the new programs and taking into account the whole picture. Although making a difference in the community is a major goal of any police department, when they introduce a new program or technology, it is important to ensure that any new programs be implemented in collaboration with the community and that sufficient time and effort is invested prior to the program's implementation to secure its proper design.

20 Years Later – Where Are We Now?

Like with many noteworthy initiatives, the degree of success can be measured years later, if not decades and it is our duty, as academics, to assess and evaluate major initiatives that were presented, over the years, as a panacea to improve police- community relations. It is beyond the scope of this chapter to focus on more than a couple of cases in order to highlight the problems, yet, it is sufficient to identify the paradigms of the concerns we need to address in the future.

In 1996 over 20 years ago Chief Sanders, a pioneer of community-based problem solving in the San Diego Police Department (SDPD), called on police agencies to use technology to improve communication with officers in the field and with other agencies, and to open a new communication channel with communities they serve (NIJ report 1996). However, in 2017 it has been reported that the SDPD needs a boost in morale, and new leadership that will inspire young police officers. The department has suffered some blows, including police officers being convicted of misconduct, the department being sued for racism by one of its own and being found to have racial disparities in traffic stops. Furthermore, the San Diego Police Department struggles with the inability to recruit qualified candidates, and it has been stated that the current Chief, Shelley Zimmerman must take personal responsibility for the failures of the SDPD not being able to recruit and retain an adequate number of police officers. She was criticized for lack of actions that goes beyond the ability to help communities solve their problems, to being effective in solving problems within her own department. When Zimmerman switched the blame to accuse the media and others, it thwarts SDPD's ability to identify the real problems (Bowser 2017).

Yet, another department that back in 1996 championed inclusion of technology, in order to improve the quality of police community relations, was the second largest police department in the United States, the Chicago Police Department (CPD). With the advent of the Information Collection for Automated Mapping (ICAM) the CPD hoped that officers who will have access to information they need when and where they need it and whenever appropriate, would share it with the trusted community members to help them identify and solve problems and thus improve police-community relations.

However, in 2017, in perhaps the most damning, sweeping critique ever of the Chicago Police Department, the U.S. Department of Justice concluded that the city's police officers are poorly trained and quick to turn to excessive and even deadly force, most often against blacks and Latino residents, without facing consequences. The 164-page report, the product of more than a year of investigation, painted the picture of a department flawed from top to bottom, although many of the problems it cited have, for decades, been the subject of complaints from citizens, lawsuits by attorneys and investigations by news organizations (Meisner et al. 2017). Thus, despite the high expectations from 1996, once again, the advents in technology have not proved to be sufficient in improving police-community relations. It came as no surprise to one of the authors of this chapter, as she has identified the problems with the CPD already in 2001 (Haberfeld 2002), while analyzing the CPD' s CAPS training program that was aimed at improving police-community relations yet, ignored the basic hurdles in obstacles in the implementation of the tenets of Community Oriented Policing, These basic problems are identified in the last part of this chapter and should be considered when one ponders about the pros and cons of various technological innovations and their ultimate impact on police-community relations.

Community Oriented Policing and Technology in 2017– What Do We Need to Consider?

When pondering about the benefits of technology we need to first and foremost address the concept of "universal values". It is just too often assumed that policing a given community is subject to a set of universal values and all it takes to improve police-community relations is to improve the communication process between these two entities, and when it comes to technology simply provide both parties with more efficient tools to report misconduct and respond to the call for service in a speedy manner. In reality, things are just much more complicated. While many of us would agree that killing a person, in a premeditated manner, or physically abusing a child should constitute some examples of these universal values, the truth is that in many communities, practices of genital mutilation, honour killings or child abandonments are not considered as horrific as many of us might think and, on the contrary, members of these communities would find such behaviours as acceptable and certainly not subject to report to the local law enforcement. We have seen examples of such conduct in the United States and some European countries (Haberfeld 2018).

Haberfeld (2018) identified three interconnected circles that represent the problems inherent in police-community relations, be it from the standpoint of (1) lack of universal values, (2) lack of trust in officers' integrity or simply (3) lack of clarity on the officers part as to what to enforce and how to use their discretion in a way that does not conflict with the local laws and ordinances but, at the same time, does not alienate various communities that are either active or passive supporters of illegal activities, from children mutilations to terrorist activities.

Finally, what we truly need to consider, while pondering the values of various technological innovations, are the hearts and the minds of the communities and the officers charged with their safety and security. The question of how to buy the minds and hearts of individuals who support various illegal activities, based on their traditions, philosophical views or simple fear, does not have an easy answer. It is however certain that police officers' unquestioned integrity, hiring and training standards must be taken into consideration, before we invest too much time and resources into development of various technological tools that, despite their obvious technical advantages, do not take into consideration the complexity of police work and all the involved stakeholders.

Thus, it only makes sense that the final paragraph of this chapter should restate the concerns of the 1996 conference attendees, first to provide an adequate and properly designed training to officers who will be eventually asked to make use of various technological tools and innovations on a daily basis is of paramount importance and second, building and maintaining sustainable partnerships between different stakeholders is a key to the success of numerous technology-facilitated community policing programs and initiatives. For that purpose, law enforcement agencies should reach out to as many audiences as possible, at the same time as they are considering various new technological advances, to be able to gauge the communities' interests, concerns and overall attitude and readiness for collaboration and cooperation.

References

Bowser, C. (2017). SDPD retention problem comes from within. Retrieved on January 11, 2018 from: http://www.voiceofsandiego.org/topics/opinion/sdpds-retention-problem-comes-within

Goldsmith, V., McGuire, P. G., Mollenkopf, J. B., & Ross, T. A. (1999). *Analyzing crime patterns: Frontiers of practice*. Thousand Oaks, CA: Sage Publications.

Haberfeld, M. R. (2002). *Critical issues in police training*. Upper Saddle River, NJ: Prentice Hall Publishing.

Haberfeld, M. R. (2018, 3rd edition). *Critical issues in police training*. New York, NY: Pearson Custom Publishers.

Lafrance, A. (2015). *How many websites are there?* The Atlantic. Retrieved on January 11, 2018 from: https://www.theatlantic.com/technology/archive/2015/09/how-many-websites-are-there/408151

Meisner, J., Sweeney, A., Hinkel, D. & Gorner, J. (2017). Retrieved on Janaury 11, 2018 from:http://www.chicagotribune.com/news/local/breaking/ct-chicago-police-justice-department-report-20170113-story.html.

National Institute of Justice. (1996). Technology for Community Policing. Conference Report.

Northrop, A., Kraemer, K. L., & Kig, J. L. (1995). Police use of computers. *Journal of Criminal Justice, 23*(30), 259–275.

Roth, J., et al. (1994). National evaluation of the cops program title I of the 1994 Crime Act. Series. NCJ.

Welch, E. W., & Fulla, S. (2005). Virtual interactivity between government and citizens. The Chicago Police Department's citizen ICAM application demonstration case. *Political Communication, 22*(2), 215–236.

Open Access This chapter is licensed under the terms of the Creative Commons Attribution 4.0 International License (http://creativecommons.org/licenses/by/4.0/), which permits use, sharing, adaptation, distribution and reproduction in any medium or format, as long as you give appropriate credit to the original author(s) and the source, provide a link to the Creative Commons license and indicate if changes were made.

The images or other third party material in this chapter are included in the chapter's Creative Commons license, unless indicated otherwise in a credit line to the material. If material is not included in the chapter's Creative Commons license and your intended use is not permitted by statutory regulation or exceeds the permitted use, you will need to obtain permission directly from the copyright holder.

Chapter 11
Policing the Community Together: The Impact of Technology on Citizen Engagement

Ben Brewster, Helen Gibson, and Mike Gunning

Introduction

At the core of engagement, and similarly the idea of 'community' as a whole, is the concept of social capital (Huysman and Wulf 2004). Social capital is a form of economic and cultural capital in which social interaction is vital, and in which social transactions are marked by cooperation, reciprocity and trust (Flora 1997), and where goods, services and interventions are produced in service of common goals. The concept of community policing is underlined by the exchange of social capital between the Police, other statutory and non-statutory organisations, citizens, communities and interest groups in pursuit of social cohesion and the collective efficacy that enables citizens and groups to participate in shaping the contexts and communities to which they belong and with whom they engage (Sampson and Raudenbush 1999). This exchange relies heavily on community participation, built upon trust and confidence in, and legitimacy of, those participating organisations and individuals. While the concepts of trust, confidence and legitimacy themselves are not inherently complex, they are values which are hard to foster, maintain and measure as the socio-political contexts and interactions that shape them are often multifaceted, fragile and sensitive to change.

The concept of community policing itself has been discussed as an extension of the 'social contract' that exists between police and citizens (van der Giessen et al. 2017), placing additional requirements and demands on both parties. From a policing perspective, this requires the acceptance of citizens and communities as a partner in local safety and security, and from the perspective of those citizens an acceptance of the police's role within their communities. But what is community

B. Brewster (✉) · H. Gibson · M. Gunning
CENTRIC – Centre of Excellence in Terrorism, Resilience, Intelligence and Organised
Crime Research, Sheffield Hallam University, Sheffield, UK
e-mail: B.Brewster@shu.ac.uk; H.Gibson@shu.ac.uk; M.Gunning@shu.ac.uk

© The Author(s) 2018
G. Leventakis, M. R. Haberfeld (eds.), *Societal Implications of Community-Oriented Policing and Technology*, SpringerBriefs in Criminology,
https://doi.org/10.1007/978-3-319-89297-9_11

policing? While the term is omnipresent in across western policing discourse, an agreed and accepted definition of what it actually entails remains elusive (Cordner 1998). Despite this continued ambiguity, the core philosophy of community polic-ing, and thus a common thread across all of its contemporary manifestations, can be distilled to focus on those activities which seek to forge working partnerships between the police and communities (Peak and Glensor 1996).

While working in partnership with the community is a fundamental precept of community policing, actually forging and maintaining these relationships is a more complex and sensitive process than is often acknowledged. Different groups and communities are often so defined by the socio-cultural and socio-economic contexts that bring them together, meaning the requirements, in terms of enablers and barri-ers to successful collaboration, are disparate from one to the next, with no one-size-fits-all approach that can be implemented holistically. Moreover, community policing is a paradigm shift away from the normality of traditional police practice, meaning officers are often ill-equipped to overcome the unwillingness of communi-ties' to work with them and foster the working relationships which are so funda-mental to the success of the approach (Sarre 1997). Thus, the challenge of working with communities that are considered disadvantaged or maligned is further accentu-ated by these factors, requiring organisational and cultural changes to foster engage-ment with the public and ultimately empower communities to participate in efforts to tackle local crime-related problems (Cameron and Laycock 2002).

Inclusion, Participation and Engagement

Le Dantec (2016) conceptualises the idea of 'Publics'. That is a collective group of people who are enlisted by a common set of shared issues, values or ideals and the interventions being taken against them. In community policing, we can appropriate this concept of publics to refer to the disparate communities with which the core values and prerequisites for collaboration between them and the police are missing or underdeveloped. These groups, are so defined by the individuals, and individual con-texts, that reside within them. While the term 'stakeholder' is often used to describe the individuals and groups with interests or concerns around a particular issue, here we move towards the use of implicated actors as a means of representing the balance of power, or lack of, that often exists within these contexts. These implicated actors are those individuals and communities who are physically present, but for whatever reason – and there can be many, are marginalised and/or silenced, and those who are not present physically – but are the targets of others' work (Le Dantec 2016).

Age, gender and socio-economic status can have huge implications when deter-mining the factors that impact upon levels of social inclusion (Livingstone and Helsper 2007). These factors can have equally significant impacts upon the levels of digital inclusion, that is the individuals ability to access and use ICTs (particularly the internet) to do things that aid them day-to-day (Madon et al. 2009). The importance of digital inclusivity within the wider, more holistic concept of social inclusion only becomes transparent when we begin to consider how individuals from different contexts make appropriate use of ICTs to impact activities in their daily lives. Digital inclusion is not just a matter of access, but also one of capability, and whether the individual in question has the prerequisite skills to leverage the ICTs in question, and the knowledge of how and when to best make use of it (Faulkner and Kleif 2003; Thomas and Wyatt 2000) The concept of inclusion from a digital perspective goes beyond the notion of accessing resource, it extends to and is dependent upon the social relations that ICTs assist in the facilitation of.

Technological Interventions for Community Participation and Engagement

The use of the UNITY mobile app as a means of community engagement, the primary case study discussed later in this chapter, is far from the first instance of ICTs being used to bridge gaps between communities and the statutory and non-statutory organisations that offer support to particular problems. A prominent example comes from the 'National Ugly Mugs' (NUM) scheme[1] designed to support sex workers in the UK. The scheme, born from the UK Network of Sex Projects, allows users, primarily sex-workers themselves, to anonymously report dangerous individuals that a believed to pose a risk or threat. Information reported through the scheme is then shared with other sex-workers. The same information is then passed on, providing the user consents, to the police. The project has been recorded as a success in both providing immediate protection to sex-workers and as a valuable resource to enrich the police's intelligence picture on crimes against them (Laing et al. 2013). Despite this, tensions between sex-workers and police remain high as sex-work remains illegal in the UK, despite widespread support for decriminalisation from some quarters (Grenfell et al. 2016). While the NUM scheme has been a relative success in circumventing the tradition of mistrust between the sex-work community and the police, there is still a visible divide between the two, and the reporting of violent and serious offences to the police by workers is still extremely patchy. This is often as a result of increases in law enforcement activity targeting the sex-work community, including raids on known premises and strict solicitation legislation that is present across some areas of the UK. Furthermore, the varied nature and scope of sex-work means the scheme is mostly used by indoor workers, with those engaging in street based solicitation, often considered to be some of the most at-risk individuals, missing out as a result of low levels of digital access, itself a consequence of their own socio-economic and socio-cultural precarity (Kinnell 2008).

Le Dantec (2016) also situates technological design interventions towards vulnerable communities, in this case around homelessness, and the relationship

---

[1] National Ugly Mugs scheme, https://uknswp.org/um/

between the service providers and their clients (Le Dantec 2012), towards under-standing the gulf between what is required for technological adoption, a process far beyond the provision of technological access (Le Dantec et al. 2011). Major events also often bring communities together, highlighting the need for cooperation and communication between different the stakeholders within them. In particular, events such as flooding, earthquakes and other disasters that directly affect specific com-munities and result in the displacement of people from their homes require effective communication to guide people towards assistance and support services. Although social media has been examined and heralded as a possible solution to this problem (Jin et al. 2011; Veil et al. 2011) the lack of a centralised service often makes the response somewhat disjointed. However, a community's resilience to disaster is often dependent on the strength of its existing social capital and thus embedding this capital before a disaster takes place is essential in fostering a more resilient response (McNulty and Rennick 2013).

Existing community engagement platforms include Nextdoor.[2] Nextdoor is an online platform which brings geographic communities together to discuss local issues, as well as offering help, support and advice to those who ask for it. In the US, Nextdoor has already been touted as a community policing tool (Waddell 2016), providing a means where public agencies, not just the police, can register and con-tribute to local community issues. However, it has been noted that such a tool has the potential to amplify community tensions or heighten awareness of crime and thus increase fear. Privacy concerns also factor in people's use of the site. These concerns cover issues ranging from knowing when property is empty and thus vul-nerable to robbery, to those surround data protection around how Nextdoor itself makes use of its users data (Masden et al. 2014). The Police have also debated the idea of using their own dedicated mobile application, but functions are often limited to accessing information around crime hotspots and local police information. Police-driven applications also suffer from their direct association with the police themselves. Their uptake is reliant on the presence of an existing culture of collabo-ration and participation within the communities using them. Moreover, in areas where these prerequisite relationships do not exist, users may fear being labelled as informants or have concerns about how their personal data may be used (Bullock 2017). Uptake in the use of these applications often reflects and even amplifies existing behaviours, cultural perceptions and trust relationships that communities have with the police. Community driven apps may be seen as having increased legitimacy compared to those imposed upon the public by statutory organisations. While the potential utility and value of mobile applications as a vector for participa-tion and engagement across groups of implicated actors is clear and apparent, this should not be confused with any presumption that these mechanisms serve as a vehicle for enhanced participation and engagement. In fact, digital inclusion and participation do not necessarily reflect, or culminate in an increase in, the broader concept of social inclusion. In a study of homelessness in Edinburgh, Buré (2006) asserted that despite regular access to ICTs among the homeless population, the

---

[2] Nextdoor, https://nextdoor.com/